Cognitive-Behavioral Stress Manage
for Individuals Living with HIV

FERMOY UNIT
N.W.M.H.F.T. NHS
QUEEN ELIZABETH HOSPITAL
GAYTON ROAD
KING'S LYNN
NORFOLK
PE30 4ET

Cognitive-Behavioral Stress Management for Individuals Living with HIV

Facilitator Guide

Michael H. Antoni • Gail Ironson • Neil Schneiderman

OXFORD
UNIVERSITY PRESS

2007

OXFORD

UNIVERSITY PRESS

Oxford University Press, Inc., publishes works that further
Oxford University's objective of excellence
in research, scholarship, and education.

Oxford   New York
Auckland   Cape Town   Dar es Salaam   Hong Kong   Karachi
Kuala Lumpur   Madrid   Melbourne   Mexico City   Nairobi
New Delhi   Shanghai   Taipei   Toronto

With offices in
Argentina   Austria   Brazil   Chile   Czech Republic   France   Greece
Guatemala   Hungary   Italy   Japan   Poland   Portugal   Singapore
South Korea   Switzerland   Thailand   Turkey   Ukraine   Vietnam

Published by Oxford University Press, Inc.
198 Madison Avenue, New York, New York 10016

www.oup.com

Oxford is a registered trademark of Oxford University Press

Library of Congress Cataloging-in-Publication Data
Antoni, Michael H.
Cognitive-behavioral stress management for individuals living with HIV :
facilitator guide / Michael H. Antoni, Gail Ironson, Neil Schneiderman.
p. cm. — (TreatmentsThatWork)
Includes bibliographical references.
ISBN 978-0-19-532791-5
1. Cognitive therapy. 2. HIV-positive persons—Mental health. 3. AIDS
(Disease)—Patients—Mental health. 4. Stress (Psychology)—Prevention.
[DNLM: 1. HIV Infections—complications. 2. Stress, Psychological—
prevention & control. 3. Cognitive Therapy—methods. 4. HIV
Infections—psychology. 5. Stress, Psychological—etiology.
WM 172 A6345c 2007] I. Ironson, Gail H. II. Schneiderman, Neil.
III. Title. IV. Treatments that work.
RC489.C63A58 2007
616.89′142—dc22   2007014361

9 8 7 6 5 4 3 2 1

Printed in the United States of America
on acid-free paper

About Treatments *ThatWork*™

Stunning developments in healthcare have taken place over the last several years, but many of our widely accepted interventions and strategies in mental health and behavioral medicine have been brought into question by research evidence as not only lacking benefit, but perhaps inducing harm. Other strategies have been proven effective using the best current standards of evidence, resulting in broad-based recommendations to make these practices more available to the public. Several recent developments are behind this revolution. First, we have arrived at a much deeper understanding of pathology, both psychological and physical, which has led to the development of new, more precisely targeted interventions. Second, our research methodologies have improved substantially, such that we have reduced threats to internal and external validity, making the outcomes more directly applicable to clinical situations. Third, governments around the world and healthcare systems and policymakers have decided that the quality of care should improve, that it should be evidence-based, and that it is in the public's interest to ensure that this happens (Barlow, 2004; Institute of Medicine, 2001).

Of course, the major stumbling block for clinicians everywhere is the accessibility of newly developed evidence-based psychological interventions. Workshops and books can go only so far in acquainting responsible and conscientious practitioners with the latest behavioral healthcare practices and their applicability to individual patients. This new series, Treatments *ThatWork*™, is devoted to communicating these exciting new interventions to clinicians on the frontlines of practice.

The manuals and workbooks in this series contain step-by-step detailed procedures for assessing and treating specific problems and diagnoses. But this series also goes beyond the books and manuals by providing ancillary materials that will approximate the supervisory process in assisting practitioners in the implementation of these procedures in their practice.

In our emerging healthcare system, the growing consensus is that evidence-based practice offers the most responsible course of action for the mental health professional. All behavioral healthcare clinicians deeply desire to provide the best possible care for their patients. In this series, our aim is to close the dissemination and information gap and make that possible.

This facilitator guide, and the companion workbook for clients, is designed to help individuals living with HIV deal with stress and improve quality of life. As the AIDS epidemic continues, it is important to serve the needs of this population. An estimated 39.5 million people are living with HIV worldwide, with approximately 1.2 million in the United States. As stress has been shown to impair the immune system, stress management is crucial for HIV-infected individuals, who are at high risk for decreased immune functioning.

This comprehensive group program combines Cognitive-Behavioral Stress Management (CBSM) techniques with a wide array of relaxation methods. Participants build on their stress management skills every session, increasing their awareness of stress and their ability to cope with stress. Discussion and examples are set in the context of living with HIV. During each session, participants practice a relaxation technique under the guidance of the group leaders. By the end of the program, participants' relaxation repertoire includes breathing, progressive muscle relaxation, imagery, autogenic training, and meditation.

This program provides proven methods to manage stress and induce relaxation. Its two-sided approach is particularly useful, offering participants the maximum benefit. Those working with HIV-infected individuals to reduce their stress levels and improve their quality of life will find this an indispensable guide.

David H. Barlow, Editor-in-Chief,
Treatments *That Work*™
Boston, Massachusetts

Acknowledgments

This facilitator guide and accompanying workbook were developed over years of theoretical and empirical research conducted in the Behavioral Medicine Research Center at the University of Miami Department of Psychology. Initially, as part of Miami's Center for the Biopsychosocial Study of AIDS, a National Institute of Mental Health (NIMH)-funded center, our behavioral medicine research team examined relations among stress, neuroendocrine, and immunologic patterns in seronegative and asymptomatic HIV-seropositive gay men. Subsequently, with NIMH-supported program project support, individual research project support, and research training grant support, our focus was expanded to examine symptomatic as well as asymptomatic HIV-infected individuals, long-term survivors of AIDS, and HIV-infected minority women. The culmination of this work was the development of an intervention—Cognitive-Behavioral Stress Management (CBSM)—for stress-related processes in order to facilitate quality of life and optimal disease management in HIV-infected persons. We are indebted to the NIMH for these years of support that allowed us to develop a theoretically based and empirically supported CBSM intervention for HIV-infected persons.

We are also indebted to the many faculty, scientists, clinicians, postdocs, and graduate and undergraduate students at the University of Miami who facilitated the body of research that has been conducted with this intervention. The early developmental work was led by ourselves, along with Drs. MaryAnn Fletcher, an immunologist; Mahendra Kumar, a biochemist; and Nancy Klimas, an internist with a specialization in infectious disease. We were aided considerably in this work by several talented graduate students and postdocs, including, among others, Nancy Costello, Dean Cruess, Stacy Cruess, Elizabeth Dettmer, Brian Esterling, Andrea Friedman, Kristin Kilbourn, Susan Lutgendorf, Lisa McGuffey,

---

Frank Penedo, Deidre Pereira, Tammy Sifre, Kathleen Starr, Constance West, Jesse Williams, Teresa Woods, and Marc Zuckerman.

For their involvement in later studies, we are indebted to Drs. Ron Duran, Mary Ann Fletcher, Nancy Klimas, Suzanne Lechner, Maria Llabre, Kevin Maher, Schawn McPherson-Baker, and Frank Penedo and Deidre Pereira (both then faculty); and graduate students and postdocs Andres Bedoya, Ilona Buscher, Adam Carrico, Aimee Danielson, Denise Dixon, Nicole Ennis, Jeff Gonzalez, Conall O'Clerigh, Rosario Morales, Michele Peake, Rachel Rose, Brenda Stoelb, Peter Theodore, and Kate Weaver.

Finally we are indebted to the many brave individuals who have faced HIV and who have given their valuable time to participate in our research program. Our initial work focused on HIV-infected gay and bisexual men due to the high prevalence that this group endured during the 1980s and early 1990s. However, shifting demographic patterns of the HIV/AIDS epidemic to women and underserved minorities have made these groups the focus of much of the later research with CBSM as we seek ways to help these populations to manage their disease. CBSM appears to have a significant role to play in the management of HIV spectrum disease for years to come.

Contents

Chapter 1 | *Introductory Information for Facilitators*

Background Information and Purpose of This Program

This intervention program was developed specifically for individuals dealing with the stress of living with human immunodeficiency virus (HIV) infection. The program combines relaxation and cognitive-behavioral techniques together into a Cognitive-Behavioral Stress Management (CBSM) intervention. The program is designed to: (a) provide individuals with information on sources of stress, the nature of human stress responses, and different coping strategies used to deal with stressors; (b) teach anxiety reduction skills, such as progressive muscle relaxation and relaxing imagery; (c) modify maladaptive cognitive appraisals using cognitive restructuring; (d) enhance interpersonal conflict resolution and communication skills via assertiveness training and anger management; and (e) increase the availability and utilization of social support networks through the use of improved interpersonal and communication skills. This specific CBSM intervention is tailored to address the issues of loss of personal control, coping demands, social isolation, and anxiety and depression—all salient for HIV-infected individuals.

This program is a 10-week structured intervention meeting once weekly for 2 to 2½ hours. Each session begins with relaxation training, including in-session practice of relaxation exercises. The second portion of each session teaches cognitive-behavioral techniques that can be interwoven with HIV-related health information (e.g., about sexual behavior, substance use, and medication adherence). One feature that distinguishes this stress management program from others is that the program is designed to be run in groups. These groups consist of up to eight HIV-infected individuals led by one or two group leaders. During the intervention group leaders: (a) act as coping role models along with group members (positive social comparisons, and use of social support for informational purposes); (b) encourage emotional expression and provide the opportunity to seek emotional and instrumental social support; (c) teach group members how to replace feelings of doubt with a sense of confidence (vulnerability changes); and (d) discourage the use of avoidance coping and encourage acceptance and reframing as coping responses.

Problem Focus

HIV, which is a retrovirus of the human T-cell leukemia/lymphoma line, is the causative agent of the acquired immunodeficiency syndrome (AIDS). HIV-infected persons are extremely vulnerable to a wide range of pathogens normally controlled by the immune system, and subsequently these individuals may contract a number of life-threatening diseases over the course of their infection. Because appropriate patient management can delay the onset of AIDS but never cure the primary infection, it is accurate to view HIV as a chronic disease.

Since there is no cure for AIDS, prevention is the major tool for limiting the spread of the disease. *Primary prevention* efforts focus on behavioral change techniques designed to avoid or decrease exposure to HIV, and include increasing availability and promoting use of condoms, and substance abuse management and treatment (Schneiderman, Antoni, Ironson et al., 1992). *Secondary prevention* efforts are designed to facilitate disease management once a person has been infected. These focus on treatments to manage HIV spectrum disease, optimize quality of life, and slow disease progression. The CBSM program described in this guide is a secondary prevention program. Other secondary prevention efforts focus on medications. During the past several years a number of pharmacologic agents have been introduced to manage symptoms and to slow HIV progression.

We have for the past 20 years systematically examined the effects of stress management in HIV infection as well as other chronic diseases (Antoni, Schneiderman, & Penedo, 2007). A major reason for developing stress management interventions for HIV-infected persons comes from our conceptualization of HIV infection as a chronic disease whose clinical course may be affected by multiple behavioral and biological factors. HIV-infected people who go on to develop AIDS are those whose immune systems have been compromised to the point that they develop complications such as acute life-threatening infections and rapidly progressing cancers. We have examined ways in which psychosocial influences such as CBSM intervention can be used to modulate psychosocial and behavioral factors known to affect the immune system in this population. From the point of view of a chronic disease model, to the extent that CBSM modifies things such as emotional distress, maladaptive coping strategies, and social isolation, it might also modulate biological factors such as certain immune system components. By diminishing the impact of psychosocial and behavioral factors on the immune system, CBSM might retard the onset of disease complications by maintaining an individual's immunologic status (e.g., T-helper cell counts) within a certain range necessary to defend against certain pathogens.

Based on the empirical observations in biobehavioral studies of cohorts of HIV-infected persons studied over several years (e.g., Leserman, 2003) we have constructed a model for behavioral intervention in HIV infection. The model specifies relationships based upon our observations that a CBSM intervention: (a) enhances adaptive coping strategies (active-involvement strategies) and decreases maladaptive coping strategies (denial, disengagement, giving up) and social isolation following an HIV+ diagnosis; (b) attenuates the distress associated with learning an HIV+ diagnosis; and (c) has a normalizing effect on adrenal hormone and immune status (Antoni, 2003a). We theorized that intervention-associated enhancement of adaptive coping strategies and social support may mediate both affective and behavioral risk changes on the one hand and immunologic changes on the other. Both behavioral (and affective) and immunologic changes may favor a normalization effect upon latent herpesvirus reactivation, which may reduce HIV reactivation and retard clinical disease progression (Antoni et al., 1995). It is also plausible that HIV-infected persons may benefit substantially from psychosocial interventions that build self-efficacy, enhance active cognitive and interpersonal coping skills, and increase the availability and utilization of social support in a supportive group environment. Subsequent increases in self-efficacy, social support, and adaptive coping may decrease depression and distress, sexual risk behaviors, and substance use, with potential related effects on immunologic and clinical health status.

Evidence Base for Group-Based CBSM Intervention

A number of laboratories across the world have tested the effects of psychosocial interventions on psychosocial outcomes in HIV-infected persons (for review, see Antoni, 2003b). Although studies using hypnosis and biofeedback have shown some effects on health behaviors, their effects on mood and physiological outcomes remain unknown. The bulk of the evidence for biobehavioral effects of psychosocial interventions in HIV-infected persons comes from studies of group-based CBSM intervention.

Throughout the development and empirical validation of the CBSM intervention for HIV-infected individuals described in this guide, our research program has focused on specific "critical points" that HIV-infected people pass through when testing the efficacy of psychosocial interventions. The rationale underlying this approach is that HIV infection comprises not only a "spectrum" of diseases, but also a spectrum of psychosocial challenges that change over time. At least five somewhat artificial critical points can be used to characterize these challenges: (a) responding to the initial diagnosis of seropositivity; (b) adjustment to being infected during the early asymptomatic period when individuals are still healthy; (c) adjustment to the experience of HIV-related symptoms that are not life-threatening but do affect the quality of life; (d) adjustment to a diagnosis of AIDS; and (e) managing a complex antiretroviral medication regimen. In each case we conducted randomized controlled trials where the CBSM intervention was delivered in groups by interventionists with at least a master's degree in clinical psychology. Patients recruited for these studies were required to be free of comorbid physical (e.g., cancer) or psychiatric conditions (e.g., psychosis) that could confound study results. Outcome and process measures included well-validated psychosocial instruments, commonly used physiological indices of stress, and immunologic and viral parameters known to reflect HIV disease status.

This empirical work has shown that HIV-infected men assigned to a 10-week CBSM intervention show decreased depressed mood and anxiety after learning of an HIV+ diagnosis (Antoni et al., 1991), mood changes that were paralleled by improved immune status (increased CD4+ T cells and CD56+ natural killer [NK] cells). Greater home practice of relaxation was related to larger psychological and immunological changes, suggesting a dose–response relationship (Antoni et al., 1991). In the weeks after learning this diagnosis, men assigned to CBSM continued to show better immune status, reflected in lower antibody concentrations against latent herpesviruses such as Epstein-Barr virus (lower antibodies indicate better immunologic control of the infection; Esterling et al., 1992). Greater increases in social support during this period were associated with greater declines in herpesvirus antibody concentrations (Antoni et al., 1996). At follow-up, distress at diagnosis, HIV-specific denial coping (five weeks post diagnosis minus pre diagnosis), and low treatment adherence (attendance for either CBSM or exercise groups, frequency of relaxation practice during the 10 weeks for those in CBSM, and doing homework for those in CBSM) all predicted faster disease progression over the next two years. Furthermore, decreases in denial and a greater frequency of relaxation home practice during the 10-week intervention period were predictive of higher CD4 cell counts and greater lymphocyte proliferative responses (the ability of T cells to multiply when challenged by pathogens) at the one-year follow-up (Ironson et al., 1994). These findings suggest that those men who attended intervention sessions regularly and broke through denial during the intervention period were most likely to show longer-term immune and health benefits (Ironson, Antoni, & Lutgendorf, 1995).

In another validation study in a cohort of HIV-infected men who had been diagnosed at least six months prior, we found that those assigned to a 10-week CBSM intervention showed decreased anxiety and depressed mood, increased use of acceptance and positive reframing coping, increased social support, and decreased antibody concentrations against herpes simplex-type 2 (HSV-2) virus (genital herpes) (Lutgendorf et al.,

1997, 1998). Greater use of acceptance and reframing and increases in reported social support explained the effects of CBSM on depressed mood, and depressed mood decreases ran in parallel with decreases in HSV-2 antibody titers. HIV-infected men in CBSM also showed decreases in the adrenal "stress" hormones cortisol and norepinephrine in 24-hour urine samples over the 10-week intervention (Antoni et al., 2000a,b) that paralleled mood changes over this period. When this cohort was followed over time we found that men assigned to CBSM showed greater indicators of immune system reconstitution (recovery) at the 12-month follow-up, as indicated by increased naïve T-helper cells (Antoni et al., 2002) and T-cytotoxic (killer) cells (Antoni et al., 2000b). Importantly, increases in each of these immune cell subpopulations were predicted by decreases in negative mood and adrenal stress hormones during the initial 10-week intervention: anxiety and norepinephrine decreases, reflecting decreased sympathetic nervous system activity, predicted greater numbers of killer T cells at follow-up (Antoni et al, 2000b), while decreases in depressed mood and the stress hormone cortisol predicted greater naïve T cells at follow-up (Antoni et al., 2005).

In a more recent trial, we tested the effects of CBSM on HIV-infected men being administered highly active antiretroviral therapy (HAART) (Antoni, Carrico, et al., 2006). We assigned men to either a pharmacist-led medication adherence condition or this same condition plus the 10-week CBSM program. Men assigned to the CBSM-plus-pharmacist condition showed greater decreases in HIV viral load (concentration of HIV RNA in the peripheral blood) over a 15-month follow-up compared to those in the pharmacist-only condition. These decreases in viral load were explained in part by the decreased depressed mood experienced by men in the CBSM-plus-pharmacist condition (Antoni et al., 2006). Depression reduction was related to the reduced use of denial coping after the CBSM intervention was completed (Carrico et al., 2006). This suggests that CBSM decreases nonproductive coping strategies such as denial to improve depressed mood and may, in turn, affect disease activity over longer periods (Antoni et al., 2006). Throughout this program of research we have found consistent evidence that this 10-week group-based CBSM intervention can modulate psychological adjustment to HIV infection and that improvements in psychosocial and neuroendocrine "stress" processes are related to alterations in immune and viral parameters that may affect health outcomes in HIV-infected men. More recent work has shown that CBSM intervention can also improve psychological functioning in HIV-infected women (Lechner et al., 2003). Ongoing work is examining the effects of CBSM on health outcomes in HIV-infected women at risk for certain opportunistic diseases, in men and women who are Spanish speakers, and among heterosexual men with HIV infection.

What Is CBSM?

The CBSM program described in this guide combines multiple types of relaxation (Bernstein & Borkovec, 1973), imagery, and other anxiety reduction techniques with commonly used cognitive-behavioral approaches such as cognitive restructuring (Beck & Emory, 1979), coping effectiveness training (Folkman et al., 1991), assertiveness training, and anger management (Ironson et al., 1989). These are all packaged in a group-based program comprising 10 weekly modules that use contemporary stressors in the lives of HIV-infected persons to enact these well-proven techniques for managing stress.

Alternative Treatments

Other Relaxation Techniques

As a result of the literature relating relaxation to anxiety reduction and improvement in immune measures (e.g., Kiecolt-Glaser et al., 1985, 1986), and because frequency of relaxation home practice was related to better immunological functioning and slower disease progression in our prior studies of HIV-infected men (Antoni et al., 1991; Ironson et al., 1994), it is worth noting that there are alternate ways of inducing relaxation. One of these is massage therapy. Ironson and colleagues (Ironson, Field, Scafidi et al., 1995) demonstrated in a nonrandomized design that HIV-infected men offered daily massage for 20 days showed a significant increase in NK cells and T-killer cells and decreases in anxiety and 24-hour urinary cortisol output, compared to men's values during the no-massage period.

Individual Treatment

The CBSM interventions evaluated by us in different cohorts of HIV-infected gay men all employed groups of up to eight participants facilitated by two group leaders. The sessions were conducted in comfortable rooms, ran about 2½ hours in duration, and met on a weekly basis over a 10-week period. While there was some variability in terms of the duration of group programs for HIV-infected persons evaluated by other research groups (range = 8–12 weeks), the number of participants, group leaders, session length, and frequency were quite similar across studies (Antoni, 2003b). Because these sessions were conducted in a group format, less is known about the effects of these sorts of techniques with HIV-infected persons when delivered as individual-based psychotherapy sessions or self-help approaches. Given the expense involved in running clinical trials of psychotherapy on an individual basis, it is likely that individual-based empirical research will not proceed until the effects of group-based programs are well established.

Other Treatment Orientations

The role of treatment orientation in psychosocial interventions for HIV-infected persons has been addressed in only a few studies. Studies comparing different 15-week group interventions using a cognitive-behavioral versus an existential/experiential orientation in asymptomatic HIV-infected gay men found that both of the psychosocial intervention conditions decreased mood disturbance and depression symptoms compared to wait-list controls (Mulder, Emmelkamp, Antoni et al., 1994). It is important to note that despite the differences in theoretical orientation both interventions were designed to reduce stress, improve coping, build social support, and encourage emotional expression. Those intervention group participants with larger decreases in a distress/depression composite between the beginning of either intervention and nine months later showed significantly less decline in T-helper cell counts over a two-year follow-up period from the beginning of the intervention (Mulder, Antoni et al., 1995). These findings suggest that while theoretical orientation may not contribute to the psychological improvements experienced by HIV-infected men participating in group-based psychosocial interventions, the magnitude of treatment-related reductions in distress (perhaps related to a greater commitment to the intervention guidelines) may predict longer-term health benefits. This interpretation seems to be in line with the findings reviewed previously (Antoni et al., 1991, for short-term effects and Ironson et al., 1994, for longer-term effects).

Outline of This Treatment Program

The overall aims, general strategies, and specific techniques of the 10-week group program are summarized in table 1.1.

The five sets of stress management techniques used in this program are cognitive restructuring, coping skills training, assertiveness training, anger management, and social support building. We spend 1 to 3 weeks training participants in the use of each of these techniques. Each topic is introduced with background information and exercises designed first to increase participants' awareness of subtle stress response processes that are addressed by the technique being taught. This step is followed by an

Table 1.1 Aims, Strategies, and Techniques for CBSM Intervention

A. Aims	B. Strategies	C. Techniques
1. Increase awareness	1. Provide information (stress responses, risk behavior) and experiences	1. Didactic and written information, self-monitoring exercises
2. Teach anxiety reduction skills	2. Relaxation	2. Progressive Muscle Relaxation, guided imagery, Autogenics, meditation, diaphragmatic breathing
3. Modify cognitive appraisals	3. Cognitive-behavioral stress management techniques	3. Cognitive restructuring, rational thought replacement
4. Build interpersonal coping skills and increase emotional expression	4. Address interpersonal conflicts and facilitate disclosure to group	4. Coping skills training, assertiveness training, anger management
5. Reduce social isolation	5. Build social support network	5. Provide group support; techniques to raise awareness of social network components

introduction to the rationale for the technique and the steps for implementing it. The balance of the session is spent applying the technique to examples of ongoing stressors in the lives of the participants. Here we employ role-playing and breakaways into dyads wherever possible to increase the interactive nature of the experience. Weekly homework assignments reinforce the techniques learned in session.

Relaxation techniques include progressive muscle relaxation (PMR), guided imagery, autogenic training, diaphragmatic breathing techniques, and various forms of meditation. Many of the relaxation scripts used in this guide are simplified versions of widely used and validated methods. Facilitators can review the full-length versions of many of these procedures in *The Relaxation & Stress Reduction Workbook* (Davis, Eshelman, & McKay, 1988) and *Guide to Stress Reduction* (Mason, 1985). Each session introduces a new technique or a more complex version of a previously introduced technique. Group leaders review the rationale and steps for implementing each of these techniques with the group. Participants spend the bulk of the relaxation portion of the session practicing relaxation exercises, which they will then repeat at home on a daily basis. By the end of the 10-week program our goal is to have provided participants a sufficient number of techniques to allow them to choose those that they are most comfortable in using.

Using a Group Format

We developed the program to be a closed, structured group intervention meeting once weekly for 2 hours over a 10-week period in groups of up to eight persons facilitated by two group leaders. See chapter 2 for more information on the logistics of running the group program. The group format allows participants the opportunity to access and benefit from certain processes that would not be available in individual psychotherapy. The most important of these are the opportunity to use group members and group leaders as coping role models (positive social comparisons), the chance to demonstrate in vivo use of social support for informational purposes, an optimal atmosphere for encouraging emotional expression, and an opportunity to seek emotional and instrumental social support from the other group members in a semipublic yet safe and confidential environment. In so doing, the true efficiency of the group format can be maximized for the purpose of modeling as well as teaching all of the previously noted components in our conceptual model for intervening with the HIV-infected individual.

Use of the Client Workbook

The workbook is designed to provide group members with an overview of the CBSM program and will aid facilitators in delivering this intervention. It contains detailed summaries of the rationale for and content of each of the 10 meetings making up the treatment. Each workbook session includes psychoeducational information about stress management techniques and basic instructions for relaxation exercises. It provides forms and worksheets for completing in-session activities designed to raise participants' level of awareness of subtle stress response processes and to practice applying stress management techniques to examples of stressors. In addition to these in-session activities, each workbook session contains a take-home activity designed to help individuals practice applying their newly learned CBSM techniques to stressors and events that occur in their everyday lives. Participants complete monitoring forms during the week and discuss their progress with relaxation practice and stress management techniques during each weekly meeting. Most forms can be photocopied from the workbook or downloaded from the Treatments *ThatWork*™ Web site at www.oup.com/us/ttw.

The workbook is divided into chapters that coincide with the 10 weekly sessions that make up the program. The workbook has been designed to continually dovetail with the *Facilitator Guide* such that the training manual contains several "toggle" points at which group leaders are instructed to incorporate actual workbook pages into the activities conducted in the group sessions. As such, all participants are instructed to bring their workbooks to every session.

Together, the *Facilitator Guide* and the *Cognitive-Behavioral Stress Management Workbook* make up the backbone of the program and should be used together in implementing the program with HIV-infected individuals.

Chapter 2 *Logistics of the Cognitive-Behavioral Stress Management Intervention Program*

Group Meetings and Program Duration

We have designed the CBSM program to be used in the context of regular (preferably weekly) group meetings supplemented by out-of-session individual activities such as relaxation practice and various self-monitoring exercises. Although we have conducted the group sessions (relaxation, stress management) in two 60- to 90-minute sessions per week, participants report to us that the preferred format is to combine the relaxation and stress management sessions into a single 2- to 2½-hour session held once weekly. We currently run all of our CBSM groups using this format. Because of the length of these sessions it is recommended that each session begin with the relaxation training portion, followed by a 15-minute break before proceeding to the stress management portion. Since the program will run for 10 weeks, it is important to establish, prior to the first group meeting, an optimal location and meeting time for all of those attending. At this point, group leaders should also probe for any prescheduled activities that may preclude a participant's ability to attend certain sessions so that appropriate readings and exercises from the workbook can be assigned in order to keep the participant "in sequence."

Group Size

The optimal size of a CBSM group is six to eight participants led by two group leaders, which will ensure a good balance of lively group interactions and group leader monitoring. The number of participants can be as low as three without the effectiveness of group interactions being diminished substantially. Groups larger than eight participants are not recommended, as the two group leaders' ability to effectively monitor various elements of the program may be compromised. Although certain in-session activities do utilize small group discussions and role-play dyads, it is not critical to have even-numbered size groups, since a group leader can be employed to form a dyad in most any session.

Closed Group Format

Since the CBSM program uses a programmed sequence of relaxation-based and stress management techniques that progressively build on one another, it is important that all group members learn the techniques in a specific order. Due to this requirement it is necessary to run the CBSM sessions as a closed group format. While it is reasonable, on occasion, to allow a participant to join the group meetings in the second weekly session, or to miss a meeting later in the program, it is not advisable to run the program as an open-ended "revolving" group with new members joining throughout the 10-week period.

Sequence of the CBSM Sessions

One of the most frequent questions we receive from group leaders running the CBSM program is to what degree they should deliver the intervention as a sequenced and structured set of techniques versus tailoring the program to the individual needs of group members. Because the program incorporates many different relaxation-based and stress management techniques in the relatively short period of 10 weeks it is essential that group leaders remain "on track" within sessions and across the 10-session sequence. At the same time, however, it is critical that participants be given the opportunity in each session to apply each newly learned CBSM technique to stressful areas of their own lives and to go back and review with group leaders any material that they did not fully grasp from prior modules.

We designed the program based on the hypothesis that relaxation-based and stress management techniques can be most effectively introduced in a logical order progressing from simple, unitary procedures to combinations of different procedures. For example, progressive muscle relaxation training is conducted over a number of sessions, increasing in complexity with each session. In the first session, 16 muscle groups are used. In the second session, participants continue with progressive muscle relaxation, but with only eight muscle groups. In the third session, the number of muscles is further reduced to four. In the fourth session, passive progressive muscle relaxation is introduced and combined with guided imagery. Over the course of the 10-week program participants "progress" from active muscle relaxation to more passive muscle relaxation techniques, then to unitary guided imagery experiences combined with relaxation exercises, and finally to imagery procedures integrated with diaphragmatic breathing, autogenics, and meditation.

We also instruct participants in the use of stress management techniques in a pre-arranged sequence based on a four-component theory that classes stress management processes into (1) awareness-raising activities, (2) appraisal activities, (3) coping response activities, and (4) coping resource activities. We have reasoned that in addition to learning all of the most effective CBSM techniques available, participants should understand the ways in which these four stress management processes are interrelated and the ways that they can be used in sequence during stressful transactions. The stress management techniques progress from simpler awareness-raising exercises to more complex cognitive-behavioral techniques such as cognitive restructuring, coping skills training, anger management, and assertiveness training. Here the "progression" moves not only from simpler to more complex strategies, but also (in accordance with our stress management theory) from more cognitive activities (appraisals), to behavioral activities (coping), and finally to interpersonal activities (anger expression, assertive communication, and social support accessing).

Maintenance Sessions

We have used monthly maintenance sessions after the completion of our 10-week program and found that participants are eager to attend such meetings. At these sessions they are encouraged to:

■ Describe the recent stressors that they have experienced and the degree to which they have been able to use CBSM strategies to deal with them

- Describe alternative coping strategies that they have developed and factors that seem to facilitate or obstruct their ability to cope successfully with stressors

- Self-monitor their perceived stress levels and relaxation practice frequency on a weekly basis and to record this information on the Daily Self-Monitoring Sheets that are turned in at each maintenance session

At the end of the 6-month maintenance period, we offer group members the opportunity to continue meeting on a monthly basis and provide one of the group leaders to conduct these sessions, which are structured as an open group. We also refer group members to local support organizations that have ongoing groups for HIV-infected individuals. Reports from these maintenance sessions indicate that the participants are utilizing newly learned cognitive restructuring techniques, assertiveness skills, and relaxation exercises; that they are experiencing improvements in interpersonal relationships and lower perceived stress levels; and that they enjoy the opportunity to report to the group on their frustrations and progress in using these strategies to cope with stressors.

Training Group Leaders

During the developmental and field trial stages of the program we have used master's-level (less than 2 years of clinical training) clinical health psychology graduate students and clinical psychology faculty to conduct groups. Although the program has never been tested with other health-care professionals (e.g., nurses, licensed clinical social workers), this manual has been designed to be an appropriate guide for any professional with prior group therapy and mental health training experience. In some cases, non-mental healthcare professionals who have had extensive experience in conducting focused patient support groups may also be able to implement the program with relative ease.

We recommend that all prospective group leaders complete a training sequence conducted over a 10-week period prior to implementing the program, guided by the *Facilitator Guide* and supervised by a licensed mental health professional. In our prior work this training sequence comprised intensive in-class training in progressive muscle relaxation, guided imagery, diaphragmatic breathing, autogenics, meditation, cognitive restructuring, coping skills training, anger management, and assertiveness training; audiotaped role-playing exercises with other trained group leaders that were subsequently reviewed for adherence to protocol by licensed clinical supervisors; and readings on relevant topics such as counseling issues in HIV-infected clients, psychosocial and sociocultural factors associated with sexual risk behaviors and substance use in HIV-infected individuals, and the nature of the group therapy process.

Once a CBSM group commences at our institution all sessions are audiotaped (with subjects' informed consent), and these are reviewed by two licensed mental health professionals on a weekly basis. The group leaders meet with these two individuals on a weekly basis to review the events of each session. On the basis of audiotapes of each session and weekly face-to-face supervision, adherence to the weekly treatment modules (as outlined in the treatment manual) is monitored. These are the criteria and training procedures that we have been using over the years in our studies of HIV-infected persons. Clinicians choosing to use the program may have other means for ensuring the validity of the delivery of this intervention.

Relaxation Scripts and Use of Audio Recordings

Many of the relaxation scripts used in this guide are simplified versions of widely used and validated methods. Facilitators can review the full-length versions of many of these procedures in *The Relaxation & Stress Reduction Workbook* (Davis, Eshelman, & McKay, 1988) and *Guide to Stress Reduction* (Mason, 1985).

For relaxation exercises, we recommend making audio recordings of the facilitators reciting the relaxation scripts to be used in session. Copies should be distributed to participants to use during their home practice. This will facilitate effective repetition of these exercises, particularly those involving imagery.

Chapter 3

Session 1: Introduction to the Program / Stressors and Stress Responses / Progressive Muscle Relaxation for 16 Muscle Groups

(Corresponds to chapters 1 and 2 of the workbook)

Materials Needed

- Relaxation mats

- Flip chart or blackboard

- Copy of the participant workbook

- Copies of audio recording of PMR script for 16 Muscle Groups (optional)

- Copies of Daily Self-Monitoring Sheet (optional)

- Copies of Session Evaluation Questionnaire (optional)

INTRODUCTION TO THE PROGRAM

Outline

- Introduce group leaders (5 minutes)

- Present general program information (15 minutes)

- Describe the structure of the program (10 minutes)

- Conduct Getting Acquainted Exercise (20 minutes)

Introduction of Group Leaders (5 minutes)

At the beginning of the first session, take a few minutes to introduce yourselves as the group leaders. Be sure to include your professional background in your introduction. Also, provide positive reinforcement to the participants for coming to the group.

General Program Information (15 minutes)

Purpose

This program focuses on stress management techniques and relaxation skills. Explain to the group that you will be discussing ways to deal with stress in a healthy and effective manner. Most people experience some type of stressful situation every so often, some more than others do. Group members will learn skills to use in stressful work, home, or social situations that they encounter in their daily lives. The following dialogue may be helpful in your discussion:

> *You don't have to be leading a stressful life in order to benefit from these skills; they are also helpful in situations that don't seem so stressful. For example, you can apply the skills taught in this program to making decisions or communicating more effectively in all kinds of situations. So, you don't have to be under a lot of stress in order to gain something from your participation. However, you will find that at those times when you do experience stress, the techniques you will learn will help you cope.*

Next talk about what participants can expect of the group. Emphasize that this group is for them, and you will tailor it to meet their needs. Say that you are looking to have input from them on what to discuss each week within the general topic areas.

Attendance

This group program is designed to be conducted over 10 weekly sessions of approximately 2 to 2½ hours; however, this can be adjusted according to the group's needs. Set the meeting schedule and stress that it is important for participants to come to all of the sessions, as each session will build on the stress management and relaxation skills taught in the previous session.

Confidentiality

Discuss the issue of confidentiality with the group. You may want to use the following dialogue:

> Some of you have been in groups before, so you know that confidentiality is an important issue. Confidentiality is necessary so that participants can speak naturally in the group. You can feel free to talk about your own experiences or feelings, but please don't talk about other members' experiences even without using their names. If someone outside the group happens to know them, sometimes they can guess from the context who they are, and there goes the group's confidentiality. Again, outside the group, feel free to talk about your own experiences and what you are learning, but not about the experiences of others in the group. Is that something everyone can agree to?

Give participants an opportunity to talk about whom they might be prone to share with and reinforce that they are not to share information about group members with anyone outside of the group.

Structure of the Program (10 minutes)

Each session will consist of two parts. One part will cover stress management techniques and the other part will teach relaxation exercises.

Stress Management Techniques

This part of the session will usually begin with group discussion of stressful situations that individuals may encounter, everyday situations that participants in the group bring up, issues related to sexual orientation, and issues related to AIDS (such as recent medical information and social issues). Next, group leaders will introduce a new set of stress management techniques that will help group members to process and respond to stressful events in a more efficient and less "stressful" way. Participants will then engage in a number of exercises to help them to learn to apply these new techniques to challenges that arise in everyday life.

Some of the topics you will be discussing may be uncomfortable or anxiety-producing for the group and may be something some group members prefer not to talk or hear about. Tell participants in that case, they may elect to play a less active and vocal role in the group discussion. However, it is important that they attend every session, and that the group discusses these topics and concerns. If individuals are anxious or uncomfortable with a topic, work with them to learn how to handle the anxiety and reduce it so they can process the information the group is providing. The following dialogue can be used to encourage group participation:

> *Both of us leaders bring our experiences and training to the group. We also know that many of you have already done a lot of work to increase your awareness and change your attitudes in response to being HIV-infected. This program will provide you with some tools, but we haven't been through your experiences, so much of your learning will come from sharing with other group members.*

Group discussion will lead into learning new stress management techniques. The stress management techniques covered during the program are based on a central framework that emphasizes the use of cognitive-behavioral strategies to increase awareness, challenge distorted cognitive appraisals (thoughts) about stressful events, modify coping strategies, and build resources. These components are viewed as interdependent processes that build upon one another. In general, first participants must learn to be aware of their responses to stressors (e.g., their interpretations of an event), then change the way they think about the stressor, alter the way they behaviorally "cope" with the stress, and learn ways to use external resources (e.g., getting help from others) to better manage stress. Direct group members to the four components listed in the workbook or write these down on a flip chart.

Four Components of Stress Management

1. Awareness: *How we react to stress*

2. Appraisals: *What we think about stress*

3. Coping: *What we do about stress*

4. Resources: *What helps us manage stress*

You may want to mention that stress management techniques have been used with success for many emotional and physical problems, including anxiety and depression, insomnia, fears of dental treatment, diabetes, high blood pressure, headaches, heart disease, genital herpes, arthritis, and side effects of cancer chemotherapy.

The stress management techniques taught in this program require participants to practice on their own outside of the sessions. Explain to the group members that homework exercises will be assigned every week and that it is very important they complete them. You may want to use the following dialogue:

> *We need your commitment on doing the homework assignments. These will be very practical, like paying attention to your stress levels and what you say to yourself and how you feel when you're stressed. Most people find these exercises both interesting and useful. The weekly assignments are just as important as the group meetings and are necessary to help you get the most benefit from the program.*

Relaxation Training

The other component of each session will address the physiological aspects of stress through the use of relaxation exercises. The first relaxation technique, progressive muscle relaxation (PMR), will help participants to relax their muscles whenever they want to. Often people go about their daily lives with excess tension in their muscles. This tension isn't necessary for carrying out activities and sometimes results in headaches, backaches, and other discomforts. The relaxation exercises will help participants eliminate much of this excess tension and in turn may help them to feel better in general.

Later on in the program, group members will learn deep breathing techniques and relaxation self-suggestions called autogenic training, as well as some imagery and meditation techniques. The program provides participants with a variety of techniques so they can use whatever they like best in the future. Emphasize to group members that in order to benefit from the relaxation exercises, they will need to practice them regularly outside of the sessions. The extent of relaxation practice is clearly related to the maximum effectiveness of the program. You can use the following dialogue to encourage home practice:

> *Some of the techniques we introduce may be familiar to you, so that the group sessions will serve as reminders to use skills you already have. That may be especially true for those of you who have at one time or another used some relaxation skills or meditation. These skills can get rusty, and this group may give you the motivation to practice again.*

> *Once we teach you a relaxation technique, we will ask you to practice every day during the following weeks. Most people find it enjoyable to take this time to relax every day, but sometimes people have a hard time fitting it into their schedule. You will need to be sure to make time to do this every day. If you don't, you won't get the full benefit of the techniques.*

Getting Acquainted Exercise (20 minutes)

Open the group discussion with probing questions:

- "What do you hope to learn in this group?"

- "What made you interested in the program?"

- "What personal accomplishments would you like to achieve during these 10 weeks?"

Divide group members into pairs and have them conduct five-minute "interviews" with each other. Refer them to the Getting Acquainted Exercise in chapter 2 of the workbook to help them conduct their interviews.

After approximately 10 minutes, instruct each person to discuss with the group what he found out about his partner, and to state three adjectives (e.g., funny, smart, creative) that describe the interviewee. Begin the group presentations by modeling a summary of an interview with your co-leader. Allow approximately 1 minute for each group member's summary statement about his partner.

STRESS MANAGEMENT: *Stressors and Stress Responses*

Outline

- Examine stressors (10 minutes)
- Discuss the physical effects of stress (10 minutes)
- Discuss the possible health consequences of chronic stress (10 minutes)
- Assign homework (5 minutes)

Stressors (10 minutes)

Direct participants to turn to the exercise in chapter 2 of the workbook entitled "Generating a List of Stressors." Review the instructions. Give participants time to jot down responses in their workbooks and then ask for examples. Put these on the flip chart as offered. Continue the discussion by referring to the different ways stress has been defined (see the "What Is Stress?" section in the workbook). This program focuses on the definition of stress as an individual's response to events or other stimuli (i.e., stressors) that are perceived to exceed his resources or require additional actions or energy to adjust or react to. Explain to group members that various types of emotional and physical stress symptoms may result from our interaction with stressors in the environment. For instance, some people may experience anger, depression, anxiety, or other negative mood states when they are dealing with stressors. Others may experience physical symptoms such as headaches, tightness in the chest, upset stomach, or muscle tension.

Physical Effects of Stress (10 minutes)

Have participants turn to the workbook to review the section entitled "Physical Effects of Stress." Discuss the "fight-or-flight" response and review the list of physical changes that occur as part of this response. Next, give group members a few minutes to generate a list of the physical effects of stress on them using the chart in the workbook entitled "My Physical Effects of Stress." Ask group members for items on their lists and put these on the flip chart. Add items from the list of physical changes given in the workbook if not mentioned. Briefly discuss the different ways participants experience stress.

Possible Health Consequences of Chronic Stress (10 minutes)

Next, review the possible health consequences of chronic stress, including the development of atherosclerosis (hardening of the arteries), hypertension (high blood pressure), and increased risk of heart attack and stroke. Use the information presented in the corresponding section of the workbook to discuss the relationship between stress and the immune system. Probe for how participants react to learning that stress may affect their immune system in a negative way. End this section by integrating the stress–immune system relationship into the context of HIV infection as follows:

■ Stress-related immunosuppression may compound the pre-existing immunosuppression found in HIV-infected individuals. Scientific evidence for this claim is evidenced by the fact that HIV-1 shows an increased ability to infect normal human lymphocytes in culture when corticosteroids (stress hormones) are added (Antoni, 2003a,b).

■ Studies examining the effects of loneliness, marital disruption, lack of social support, bereavement, and the stress of HIV antibody testing itself have found significant relationships between these stressors and changes in hormone levels, immune function, and psychological and emotional well-being (for review of these studies see Antoni, 2003a,b).

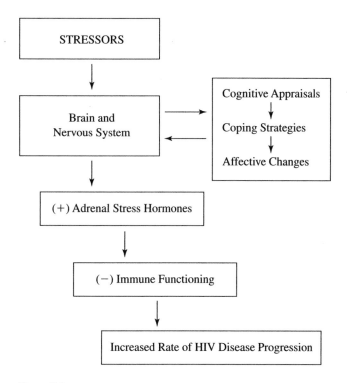

Figure 3.1

Stressors and HIV disease progression

These findings suggest that stress may affect the progression of HIV infection and increase the susceptibility of HIV-infected persons to AIDS-related infections and other diseases. Direct participants to figure 2.1 in the workbook to demonstrate the relationship between stress, immune functioning, and HIV disease progression. Explain that when we encounter stressors we first "process" them in the brain through cognitive appraisals, planned coping strategies, and affective (emotional) changes. These activities are then interpreted by the nervous system, which sends signals to endocrine glands such as the adrenals, which make stress hormones such as adrenaline and corticosteroids. Although helpful for mobilizing our bodies to deal with challenges through "fight or flight," these stress hormones also tend to dampen aspects of our immune system that are critical for combating viral infections and cancerous cells. In the case of HIV infection, stressors and the ways they are processed may contribute to accelerated disease progression through their effects on psycho-neuro-immunologic (PNI) processes.

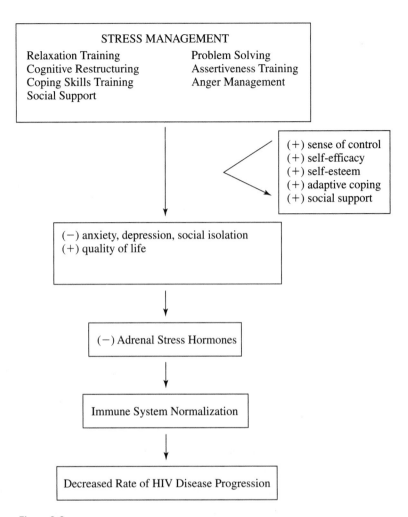

STRESS MANAGEMENT

Relaxation Training   Problem Solving
Cognitive Restructuring   Assertiveness Training
Coping Skills Training   Anger Management
Social Support

(+) sense of control
(+) self-efficacy
(+) self-esteem
(+) adaptive coping
(+) social support

(−) anxiety, depression, social isolation
(+) quality of life

(−) Adrenal Stress Hormones

Immune System Normalization

Decreased Rate of HIV Disease Progression

Figure 3.2

Stress management and HIV disease progression

Stress management and relaxation training, however, may help to offset some of the effects of such stressors and stress responses on one's psychological and physiological functioning. Techniques used to modify the ways in which we view stressful events, enhance stress coping strategies, and reduce bodily stress responses may possibly help maintain health. Refer participants to figure 2.2 in the workbook. As discussed, stress response processes can affect PNI processes relevant for HIV disease progression. The CBSM program is hypothesized to work on these processes by increasing sense of control, self-efficacy, self-esteem, adaptive coping, and social support. These changes are hypothesized to decrease negative mood states and social isolation and increase quality of life, which may lead to decreased elevations in stress hormones and normalized immune system functioning. Stress management therefore may contribute to a decreased rate of HIV disease progression.

Homework (5 minutes)

✎ Have group members monitor their stress levels at specified times each day and record on the Daily Self-Monitoring Sheet. Participants will be using a copy of this sheet every week. *Note:* If you would like to provide copies for participants, you may photocopy monitoring forms from the workbook or download multiple copies from the Treatments *ThatWork*™ Web site at www.oup.com/us/ttw.

RELAXATION TRAINING: *Progressive Muscle Relaxation for 16 Muscle Groups*

Outline

- ▣ Introduce background and rationale for progressive muscle relaxation (15 minutes)

- ▣ Conduct progressive muscle relaxation for 16 muscle groups (30 minutes)

- ▣ Assign homework (5 minutes)

- ▣ Hand out Session Evaluation Questionnaire (optional) (5 minutes)

Background and Rationale for Progressive Muscle Relaxation (15 minutes)

For the relaxation training component of the first session you will teach progressive muscle relaxation for 16 muscle groups. You can introduce this component with the following dialogue:

In the relaxation portion of the program you will learn skills to help you manage the stress you encounter in your daily life. Often, people develop physical tension when they encounter stressful and even not-so-stressful events. In this session, you will be taught a method of reducing the tension in your body. The process is called progressive muscle relaxation training or PMR. It is possible that you may have heard about it before or may have practiced it on your own. Progressive muscle relaxation training consists of learning how to tense and release various muscle groups throughout the body to decrease physical tension. By practicing this method every day you will train your muscles to relax, so less physical tension will develop.

Provide background information on PMR using the following information. PMR was first developed in the 1930s as people explored how tensing of muscles can be related to other physiological changes in the body. At the same time that muscles tense, hormones and other chemicals are released in the body. Physical changes follow, such as an increased heart rate and increased blood flow to the extremities (i.e., arms and legs). These responses can be useful if the stress we are dealing with is one that requires a physical response, such as jumping out of the way of a car or fighting off an attacker. This set of physical responses is often referred to as the "fight-or-flight" response (refer to the workbook for more information).

Usually the stresses we must deal with are not necessarily ones that require a physical response; however, the body may still react as if fighting or fleeing were adequate or appropriate responses. So the chemical and physical changes that are important for physical action still take place, but the physical action itself does not occur. As previously discussed, when these reactions are very frequent or occur over longer periods, they can have negative repercussions on physical health. Cardiovascular and immune functioning may be adversely affected so that these systems become vulnerable to damage and less able to respond to challenge. One way to prevent this is to learn how to turn off the "fight-or-flight" response. One method is to produce relaxation in the muscles, which relieves tension in the body. To conclude, you may use the following dialogue:

Basically, PMR training involves learning to tense and then relax various groups of muscles all through the body. By paying attention to the feelings generated in your body, you will learn to recognize the signs of both tension and relaxation. Being aware of your tension level and using relaxation techniques can help you to reduce the tension you may feel in everyday life. Many people find if they reduce tension, they can work more effectively or enjoy activities more and appreciate their social life to a greater extent.

Progressive Muscle Relaxation for 16 Muscle Groups (30 minutes)

Before beginning the PMR exercise, briefly review the 16 muscle groups to be used:

1,2. Lower arms

3,4. Upper arms

5,6. Lower legs

7,8. Upper legs

9. Stomach

10. Chest

11. Shoulders

12. Neck

13. Mouth, jaw, throat

14. Eyes

15. Lower forehead

16. Upper forehead

Make an important point that participants should be careful not to tense too hard; they should not feel any pain or discomfort. If at any point they feel pain or cramping, they should release their muscles immediately and tense less the following time.

Participants will be rating their stress levels on the Daily Self-Monitoring Sheet in the workbook before and after each relaxation practice. Stress levels range from 1 (lowest stress) to 7 (most stress).

PMR Script for 16 Muscle Groups

Get into a comfortable position, close your eyes, and rest quietly for a few seconds, taking some slow, deep breaths.

Lower Arms Muscle Groups

Build up the tension in your lower arms by making fists and pulling up on your wrists. Feel the tension through your lower arms, wrists, fingers, knuckles, and hands. Notice the sensations of pulling, discomfort, and tightness. Hold the tension. [Pause 10 seconds.] *Now release the tension and let your hands and lower arms relax onto the mat, with palms facing down. Focus your attention on the sensations of relaxation in your hands and arms. Feel the release from tension. Relax the muscles, and as you relax, breathe smoothly and slowly from your abdomen. Each time you exhale, think the word "relax."* [Pause 20 seconds.]

Upper Arms Muscle Groups

Now, build up the tension in your upper arms by pulling your arms back and in, toward your sides. Feel the tension in the back of your arms and radiating up into your shoulders and back. Focus on the sensations of tension. Hold the tension. [Pause 10 seconds.] *Now, release your upper arms and let them relax. Feel the difference compared with the tension. Your arms might feel heavy, warm, and relaxed. As you relax, breathe smoothly and slowly from your abdomen. Each time you exhale, think the word "relax."* [Pause 20 seconds.]

Lower Legs Muscle Groups

Now, build up the tension in your lower legs by flexing your feet and pulling your toes toward your upper body. Feel the tension as it moves up your feet into your ankles, shins, and calves. Focus on the tension spreading down the back of your lower leg into your foot, under your foot, and around your toes. Hold the tension. [Pause 10 seconds.] *Now, release the*

32

tension, letting your legs relax heavily onto the mat. Feel the difference in the muscles as they relax. Feel the release from tension, the sense of comfort, and the warmth and heaviness of relaxation. As you breathe smoothly and slowly, think the word "relax" each time you exhale. [Pause 20 seconds.]

Upper Legs Muscle Groups

Build up the tension in your upper legs by pulling your knees together and lifting your legs off the mat. Focus on the tightness in your upper legs. Feel the pulling sensations from the hip down, and notice the tension in your legs. Hold the tension. [Pause 10 seconds.] *Now, release the tension, and let your legs drop down heavily onto the mat. Let the tension fade away. Concentrate on the feeling of relaxation. Feel the difference in your legs. Focus on the feeling of comfort, and as you breathe smoothly and slowly, think the word "relax" each time you exhale.* [Pause 20 seconds.]

Stomach Muscle Group

Now, build up the tension in your stomach by pulling your stomach in toward your spine very tightly. Feel the tightness. Focus on that part of your body and hold the tension. [Pause 10 seconds.] *Now, let your stomach relax outwards. Let it go further and further. Feel the sense of warmth circulating across your stomach. Feel the comfort of relaxation. As you breathe smoothly and slowly, think the word "relax" each time you exhale.* [Pause 20 seconds.]

Chest Muscle Group

Now, build up the tension around your chest by taking a deep breath and holding it. Your chest is expanded, and the muscles are stretched around it. Feel the tension in your chest and back. Hold your breath. [Pause 10 seconds.] *Now, slowly, let the air escape and breathe normally, letting the air flow in and out smoothly and easily. Feel the difference as the muscles relax compared with the tension, and think the word "relax" each time you exhale.* [Pause 20 seconds.]

Shoulders Muscle Group

Imagine that your shoulders are on strings and are pulled up toward your ears. Feel the tension around your shoulders, radiating down into your back and up into your neck and the back of your head. Concentrate on the sensation of tension in this part of your body. [Pause 10 seconds.] *Now let your shoulders droop. Relax and let them droop further and further. Focus on the sense of relaxation around your neck and shoulders. Feel the difference in these muscles from the tension. As you breathe smoothly and slowly, think the word "relax" each time you exhale.* [Pause 20 seconds.]

Neck Muscle Group

Build up the tension around your neck by pressing the back of your neck toward the mat and pulling your chin down toward your chest. Feel the tightness around the back of your neck spreading up into the back of your head. Focus on the tension. [Pause 10 seconds.] *Now, release the tension, letting your head rest comfortably against the mat. Concentrate on the relaxation. Feel the difference from the tension. As you breathe smoothly and slowly, think the word "relax" each time you exhale.* [Pause 20 seconds.]

Mouth, Jaw, and Throat Muscle Group

Build up the tension around your mouth, jaw, and throat by clenching your teeth and forcing the corners of your mouth back into a forced smile. Feel the tightness, and concentrate on the sensations of tension. [Pause 10 seconds.] *Then, release the tension, letting your mouth drop open and the muscles around your throat and jaw relax. Concentrate on the difference in the sensations in that part of your body. As you breathe smoothly and slowly, think the word "relax" each time you exhale.* [Pause 20 seconds.]

Eyes Muscle Group

Build up the tension around your eyes by squeezing your eyes tightly shut for a few seconds. [Pause 5 seconds.] *Then, release and let the tension around your eyes slide away. Feel the difference as the muscles relax. As you breathe smoothly and slowly, think the word "relax" each time you exhale.* [Pause 20 seconds.]

Lower Forehead Muscle Group

Build up the tension across your lower forehead by frowning, pulling your eyebrows down and toward the center. Feel the tension across your forehead and the top of your head. Concentrate on the tension. [Pause 10 seconds.] *Now release, smoothing out the wrinkles and letting your forehead relax. Feel the difference as your relax. As you breathe smoothly and slowly, think the word "relax" each time you exhale.* [Pause 20 seconds.]

Upper Forehead Muscle Group

Build up the tension across your upper forehead by raising your eyebrows as high as you can. Feel the wrinkling and pulling sensations across your forehead and the top of your head. Hold the tension. [Pause 10 seconds.] *Now release, letting your eyebrows rest. Concentrate on the sensations of relaxation. Feel the difference in comparison to tension. As you breathe smoothly and slowly, think the word "relax" each time you exhale.* [Pause 20 seconds.]

Whole Body Relaxation

Now your whole body is feeling relaxed and comfortable. As you feel yourself becoming even more relaxed, count from one to five. One, letting all of the tension leave your body. Two, sinking further and further into relaxation. Three, feeling more and more relaxed. Four, feeling very relaxed. Five, feeling deeply relaxed. As you spend a few minutes in this relaxed state, think about your breathing. Feel the cool air as you breathe in and the warm air as you breathe out. Your breathing is slow and regular. Each time you breathe out, think the word "relax." [Pause 2 minutes.] *Now, count backward from five, gradually feeling yourself become more alert and awake. Five, feeling more awake. Four, coming out of relaxation. Three, feeling more alert. Two, opening your eyes. One, sitting up.*

Homework (5 minutes)

✎ Ask group members to fill out the Activity Log in the workbook on two separate days in order to identify when they have free time available so that they can schedule relaxation as a regular part of their daily routines.

✎ Have group members practice PMR for 16 Muscle Groups on a daily basis (twice a day if possible). They should record stress levels before and after each practice on the Daily Self-Monitoring Sheet. *Note:* Basic instructions for all relaxation exercises are included in the workbook. It is recommended that you provide group members with copies of audio recordings of the scripts used in session.

Session Evaluation (optional) (5 minutes)

It may be useful to give group members an opportunity to provide a written evaluation of the group at the end of each session. Having participants provide information about their likes and dislikes in the group and preferences for future activities may prove useful for group leaders in terms of structuring future groups. You can use the following questionnaire as is or use it as a guide in designing your own evaluation sheet. You may photocopy this form from the book or download multiple copies from the Treatments *ThatWork*™ Web site at www.oup.com/us/ttw.

1. What was your favorite or the most useful part of today's session? Why?

_____

_____

_____

2. What was the worst or least useful part of today's session? Why?

_____

_____

_____

For questions 3–5, please circle a number from the scale to answer each question:

3. How much do you want to come back for the next session?

$$1 \text{——} 2 \text{——} 3 \text{——} 4 \text{——} 5 \text{——} 6 \text{——} 7$$

(not at all)   (very much)

4. How much did you like this session?

$$1 \text{——} 2 \text{——} 3 \text{——} 4 \text{——} 5 \text{——} 6 \text{——} 7$$

(not at all)   (very much)

5. After completing this session, how stressed do you feel?

$$1 \text{——} 2 \text{——} 3 \text{——} 4 \text{——} 5 \text{——} 6 \text{——} 7$$

(not at all)   (very much)

6. Please give us any other comments or suggestions that you have about how we can make this session better.

_____

_____

_____

_____

Chapter 4 | *Session 2: Progressive Muscle Relaxation for Eight Muscle Groups / Stress and Awareness*

(Corresponds to chapter 3 of the workbook)

Materials Needed

- PMR script from Session 1
- Relaxation mats
- Flip chart or blackboard
- Copy of the participant workbook
- Copies of audio recording of PMR script for Eight Muscle Groups (optional)
- Copies of Thoughts, Feelings, and Physical Sensations Monitoring Sheet (optional)
- Copies of Daily Self-Monitoring Sheet (optional)
- Copies of Session Evaluation Questionnaire (optional)

RELAXATION TRAINING: *Progressive Muscle Relaxation for Eight Muscle Groups*

Outline

- Discuss home relaxation practice (5 minutes)
- Conduct PMR for eight muscle groups (20 minutes)
- Assign homework (5 minutes)

Discussion of Home Relaxation Practice (5 minutes)

Determine what factors facilitated doing relaxation exercises at home. Ask when participants were able to schedule in relaxation using the Activity Log. Review their Daily Self-Monitoring Sheets for adherence.

Identify any problems that participants are encountering with relaxation practice. Questions you may want to ask include:

■ "How often do you find you are relaxing?"

■ "Where are you practicing relaxation?"

■ "What gets in the way for you?"

■ "Do you find yourself encountering obstacles to doing relaxation?"

■ "What do you say to yourself that keeps you from taking the time to practice relaxation?"

■ "What have you done or said to help keep your commitment to relax?"

PMR for Eight Muscle Groups (20 minutes)

Tell the group that the next step in learning progressive muscle relaxation (PMR) is to combine muscle groups and do them together (for example, all the muscles in each arm or each leg) and do the exercise using fewer muscle groups. In contrast to last week, when the group learned PMR for 16 muscle groups, today they will learn to conduct relaxation using only eight. Use the same instructions and script as in Session 1, but for only these eight muscle groups:

1. Upper and lower arms

2. Upper and lower legs

3. Stomach

4. Chest

5. Shoulders

6. Neck

7. Eyes

8. Forehead (either upper or lower)

Homework (5 minutes)

✎ Have group members practice PMR for Eight Muscle Groups on a daily basis (twice a day if possible). They should record stress levels before and after each practice on the Daily Self-Monitoring Sheet.

STRESS MANAGEMENT: *Stress and Awareness*

Outline

- ▦ Review homework (5 minutes)

- ▦ Have group members complete Symptoms of Stress Checklist (5 minutes)

- ▦ Review the effects of stress (5 minutes)

- ▦ Discuss stress and awareness (15 minutes)

- ▦ Conduct awareness exercises (30 minutes)

- ▦ Assign homework (5 minutes)

- ▦ Hand out Session Evaluation Questionnaire (optional) (5 minutes)

Homework Review (5 minutes)

Determine if participants have any problems recording daily stress levels on the Daily Self-Monitoring Sheet. Problem solve around any difficulties with adherence.

Symptoms of Stress Checklist (5 minutes)

Have group members fill out the Symptoms of Stress Checklist in chapter 3 of the workbook. Discuss what is stressful in their lives and the corresponding effects of this stress. This discussion can be done in small groups with individuals reporting back to the larger group, or with the group as a whole. During this exercise, refer to the list of stressors participants generated in Session 1.

The Effects of Stress (5 minutes)

Last session, we defined stress as an individual's response to an external event that is perceived as exceeding her capacity to handle. Ask group members to turn their attention to the list of effects of stress included in the workbook. Alternatively, the main categories of this list could be put on a flip chart and be presented without the workbook. The categories are as follows:

- *Cognitive:* anxious thoughts, fearful anticipation, poor concentration, difficulty with memory

- *Emotional:* feelings of tension, worries, irritability, feelings of restlessness, inability to relax, depression

- *Behavioral:* avoidance of tasks, sleep problems, difficulty in completing work assignments, changes in drinking, eating, or smoking behaviors

- *Physical:* stiff muscles, teeth grinding, clenching fists, sweating, tension headaches, feeling faint, choking feeling, difficulty swallowing, stomachache, loss of interest in sex, tiredness, awareness of heart beating

■ *Social:* avoiding others, isolating oneself, seeking out other people, venting, getting easily irritated with others

Emphasize to the group that it is important to become aware of these various effects of stress. They can be used as cues of when better coping strategies are needed.

Discussion of Stress and Awareness (15 minutes)

Stress management consists of strategies that help us identify situations that cause stress and provide effective techniques for coping with stress. Explain to participants that many times we have no control over the occurrence of stressful situations. However, we can get control over the ways that we deal with stress, which can either increase or decrease our stress symptoms. First, though, we must become aware of how stress symptoms are affected by our thoughts and emotions.

Awareness of Automatic Thoughts

One goal of this stress management intervention is to help participants become more aware of automatic thoughts. These are the initial thoughts that we experience when we encounter familiar or unfamiliar people, events, or other stimuli. They occur so quickly that we refer to them as "automatic." They take place before we can "catch" ourselves and represent a habitual way of responding to stressful circumstances. Since these thoughts happen so fast, our emotional responses seem to come out of the blue.

The problem with these thoughts is that they are often negative and can vary in terms of their accuracy, causing us unnecessary distress. When their interpretation of events is extreme or inaccurate, we refer to them as "cognitive distortions." In later sessions, participants will learn how to modify cognitive distortions and replace them with more rational alternatives.

Tell group members that this program will help them develop awareness of:

- The situations in which they are most likely to have automatic thoughts

- Their most frequent kind of automatic thoughts

- How their thoughts are related to how they feel emotionally

- Ways in which their thoughts and corresponding feelings shape their behavior and their sense of confidence and self-esteem

Awareness of Physical Tension

One of the first steps to stress management is to increase awareness of both the obvious and subtle bodily signals of stress. Tell group members that you want them to get to know their sources of stress and to be able to identify the physical effects of stress as they are building up, so that they can start as early as possible to "nip stress in the bud."

Exercises to Increase Awareness of Physical Symptoms (30 minutes)

The following exercises are designed to help participants to increase their awareness of how stress affects their bodies.

Mental Body Scan Exercise

Use the following exercise to help participants become more skilled in detecting subtle changes in tension in their bodies. This will aid them in increasing awareness of stress-related physical symptoms and will make them more aware of physical changes that result from the use of relaxation and other stress management techniques.

In an effort to help you identify where in your body you typically experience the physical effects of stress, we are going to take you through a mental body scan. You should close your eyes, find yourself in a comfortable position, and start to become aware of how your body feels. Notice all the physical sensations occurring inside your body.

Bring your attention from the top of your head slowly down your body until you reach your toes. Become aware of any muscle tension, tightness, or feelings of discomfort. Focus your attention closely on areas where tension builds up, such as the abdomen, shoulders, back, and neck. As you conduct your body scan, you may want to ask yourself the following questions:

- *In what part of my body am I most tight?*

- *How long has this tension been there?*

- *What is going on that is causing the tension? What stress have I encountered recently? What am I thinking?*

After the exercise, ask group members about their experience. Questions to ask include:

- "Where did you notice that most of your physical tension lies?"

- "Are there certain situations that often cause you to feel physical tension in these areas?"

- "Is the tension always there, or does it come and go?"

- "What have you learned about your body that you did not know before this exercise?"

Imagery Exercise: Thoughts, Emotions, and Physical Sensations

Tell the group that it is important to realize that thoughts and emotions often lead to physical changes in the body. Identifying how one's mental and emotional experiences contribute to one's physical well-being is an important step in building awareness of the effects of stress on the body. In an effort to illustrate the connection between thoughts, emotions, and physical sensations, take the group through an imagery exercise that will enhance understanding of this concept.

Close your eyes and think of someone you love or care about a lot. [Pause] *Get a good picture of the person in your mind—her face and expression, the color of her hair and eyes, the kind of clothes she wears, how she holds herself. Imagine how her voice sounds and how she smells. Think about*

how you feel when you are with her. Become aware of the physical sensa-
tions in your body. Pay particular attention to your chest and stomach,
where we feel a lot of the sensations that are connected with our emotions.
Do you feel tight or loose? Open or closed? Do you feel warm inside or have
butterflies? Do you have a rising or sinking feeling? Take in all the sensa-
tions of your body and think about how they feel.

Go around the group and have members describe the physical sensations
they felt during the exercise. Inquire about what kinds of feelings they
were most aware of. They don't have to say anything about the person
that they imagined or who it is. Don't let people use generic descriptions
like "good," "nice," and so forth; they should use as many descriptive adjectives as possible. Encourage them to identify the sensations as de-
scriptively and idiosyncratically as they can (e.g., "like a snake curled up
in my stomach").

Optional Breathing Exercise

If any participants appear to grow anxious during this exercise, teach
breathing for calming. Have them breathe in to the count of 4, hold to
the count of 4, exhale to the count of 4, and hold to the count of 4 before breathing in again. Participants can use this to deal with any anxiety that comes up from any of the exercises used in this session.

Breathe in, 1 . . . , 2 . . . , 3 . . . , 4 . . . Hold, 1 . . . , 2 . . . , 3 . . . , 4 . . .
Breathe out, 1 . . . , 2 . . . , 3 . . . , 4 . . . And hold, 1 . . . , 2 . . . , 3 . . . ,
4 . . . [Repeat several times.] *This can be done at anytime, anywhere,*
when you are anxious and want to calm down.

Homework (5 minutes)

✎ Have group members continue to monitor their stress levels at specified times each day and record on the Daily Self-Monitoring Sheet.

✎ Instruct group members that for every stressful event that comes up
this week, they should note their automatic thoughts and emotional

and physical responses on the Thoughts, Feelings, and Physical Sensations Monitoring Sheet in the workbook.

✎ Have group members come up with examples of common everyday situations that cause them stress and record on the Thoughts, Feelings, and Physical Sensations Monitoring Sheet.

✎ Encourage group members to be aware of obvious and subtle stress signals during the week and record these on the Thoughts, Feelings, and Physical Sensations Monitoring Sheet.

Session Evaluation (optional) (5 minutes)

See example of Session Evaluation Questionnaire at the end of chapter 3.

Chapter 5

Session 3: Breathing, Imagery, Progressive Muscle Relaxation for Four Muscle Groups / Linking Thoughts and Emotions

(Corresponds to chapter 4 of the workbook)

Materials Needed

- PMR script from Session 1
- Relaxation mats
- Flip chart or blackboard
- Copy of the participant workbook
- Copies of audio recording of PMR script for Four Muscle Groups (optional)
- Copies of audio recording of imagery script (optional)
- Copies of Thoughts, Feelings, and Physical Sensations Monitoring Sheet (optional)
- Copies of Daily Self-Monitoring Sheet (optional)
- Copies of Session Evaluation Questionnaire (optional)

RELAXATION TRAINING: *Breathing, Imagery, Progressive Muscle Relaxation for Four Muscle Groups*

Outline

- Discuss home relaxation practice (5 minutes)
- Introduce diaphragmatic breathing (10 minutes)

- Conduct PMR for Four Muscle Groups (15 minutes)

- Conduct imagery and relaxation exercise (20 minutes)

- Discuss relaxation exercises (10 minutes)

- Assign homework (5 minutes)

Discussion of Home Relaxation Practice (5 minutes)

Determine what facilitates doing exercises at home or at work. Identify what interferes with practice. Review participants' Daily Self-Monitoring Sheets for adherence. Ask group members:

- "How often do you find you are relaxing?"

- "Where are you practicing relaxation?"

- "What gets in the way for you?"

- "Do you find yourself encountering obstacles to doing relaxation?"

- "What do you say to yourself that keeps you from taking the time to practice relaxation?"

- "What have you done or said to help keep your commitment to relax?"

Diaphragmatic Breathing (10 minutes)

Breathing Awareness

Breathing tends to be something we take for granted, even though it is one of the foundations of our life and well-being. When properly used, breathing can be a valuable tool for stress management, and in fact it is the simplest form of stress management available to us. Explain the concept of diaphragmatic breathing to the group using the following information.

If you ever watch a sleeping infant or a cat breathe, you will notice the abdomen slowly rising and falling with each breath. Most people rarely use such deep natural breathing in the course of their daily activities. Particularly when we become stressed, the tendency is to breathe much more shallowly in the upper sections of the lungs. This leaves us with less available oxygenation for our blood, and less opportunity for the release of tension. It is possible, however, to learn how to consciously control one's breathing. One of the goals of this program is to teach participants to purposefully utilize slower, deeper breaths in times of stress in order to help them relax and be in a better position to respond to the situation.

The diaphragm is a muscle separating the chest from the abdomen. Relaxation of the diaphragm results in contraction of the lungs, forcing air to be expelled. As you inhale, fresh, oxygenated air enters the lungs and oxygenates the blood coming from the heart to the lungs. Blood goes from the lungs back to the left side of the heart and is then pumped throughout the body to nourish each and every cell. In the capillaries blood is exchanged for cellular waste products and carbon dioxide. The blood carries these back through the heart to the lungs, where carbon dioxide is released and blood is reoxygenated and purified.

Shallow respiration makes it more difficult for blood to be fully oxygenated and for cells to receive their proper nourishment. Toxins are not removed from circulation, resulting in decreased functioning of bodily organs, less energy, and more tension. Deep diaphragmatic breaths, on the other hand, allow greater amounts of oxygen to be available for use by the body. Good breathing habits increase one's ability to handle stressors because they increase one's control over physical tension and allow one to follow up with more efficient coping strategies.

Next, teach the group diaphragmatic breathing. You can introduce the exercise with this dialogue:

> *The following exercise will enable you to learn how to breathe from the diaphragm. Like any new skill it must be practiced to seem natural. Because you have to breathe anyway, no one will know you are practicing breathing to reduce stress. You can practice diaphragmatic breathing in 30-second to 2-minute intervals—for example, while waiting for a red light or an elevator, or for someone to answer the phone.*

Diaphragmatic Breathing Exercise

Get into a comfortable position. Put one hand on your stomach and the other on your chest. Inhale slowly and watch which hand moves. Shallow breaths move the hand on the chest; diaphragmatic breaths move the hand on the stomach.

Now, slowly inhale through your nose. As you breathe in, count slowly to 4 and feel your stomach expand with your hand. Hold the breath for 4 seconds. Then slowly breathe out while counting to 4. Hold for 4 seconds before taking the next inhale.

Breathe in, 1 . . . , 2 . . . , 3 . . . , 4 . . . . Hold, 1 . . . , 2 . . . , 3 . . . , 4 . . .
Breathe out, 1 . . . , 2 . . . , 3 . . . , 4 . . . Hold, 1 . . . , 2 . . . , 3 . . . , 4 . . .
Continue breathing in this pattern for a few minutes, becoming more relaxed with every exhale. [Pause for a few minutes.]

Now, slowly let your breathing return to its normal rhythm.

Instruct group members to practice diaphragmatic breathing two times a day. At first, they may want to practice when they are relaxed and will not be disturbed. Once they become more skilled, however, they can begin to practice at other places and times during the day. Remind them that this skill can be used without anyone even noticing.

PMR for Four Muscle Groups (15 minutes)

In this session the number of muscle groups for progressive muscle relaxation is further reduced to four. Tell participants that with practice, they can achieve the same general relaxation with four muscle groups as they did with 16 or eight. If they are still having difficulty achieving relaxation with PMR, they may want to continue practicing with the 16 and eight muscle group versions at home.

Following the same instructions and script as in Session 1, conduct the PMR exercise for these four muscle groups:

1. Stomach

2. Chest

3. Shoulders

4. Forehead (either upper or lower)

Tell participants that for their home practice they can substitute or add other muscle groups in which they experience a lot of tension.

Imagery and Relaxation (20 minutes)

Explain to participants that mental images of varying sorts contribute in large measure to the production of our emotional states. For example, when we focus on unpleasant situations, circumstances, or people in our environment, we often feel agitated, tense, upset, and uncomfortable. Conversely, when we focus our attention on pleasant images (e.g., nature scenes, people we love) we generally feel calm, peaceful, and relaxed. Thus, during the course of relaxation training participants will practice inducing relaxation responses through the use of imagery.

You might want to tell group members that although during the imagery exercises you will be suggesting pleasant scenes for them to imagine, they can alter or change the scenes as needed to meet their individual preferences. In fact, it is especially important when participants practice these exercises at home that they make use of relaxing scenes and imagery that hold special significance for them. Individualizing these relaxation programs will allow group participants to generalize the relaxation experiences to various stressful experiences in their environment, and avoid reliance on relaxation tapes, which often do not generalize to all situations.

Ask participants to find themselves in a comfortable position on the mat, breathe naturally, and simply allow their minds to drift and gradually become part of the relaxing scenes that they are being asked to imagine. Instruct participants who have distracting thoughts to simply allow these thoughts to float through their minds and then watch the thoughts float up and out of their heads just as if the thoughts were bubbles drifting up toward the sky. Explain to participants that although some people have difficulty with these exercises at first, they are easily learned, and with continued practice the experience will become more relaxing and enjoyable.

Beach Script (with Alternative Lake Imagery)

Prior to relaxation, describe the imagery scene to group members and determine whether this is something that they feel they can relate to and enjoy. If participants do not show interest in a given imagery scene, substitute an alternative imagery scene of their own choosing. There exist a variety of resources (e.g., Davis, Eshelman, & McKay, 1988) providing such imagery scenes, and these should be consulted as needed. What follows is a general form that can be used to introduce the idea of relaxing imagery. You may want to expand on the script as time allows.

Note: Although this oceanfront beach imagery scene is usually quite popular with participants, some individuals may not relate to or may have difficulty with this or any of the later imagery scenes provided in this manual. For example, some group members may have never visited the ocean and may not feel able to clearly imagine such a scene. Thus, an alternative lakeside imagery is provided, as most people have at one time or another spent time at a lake and can easily imagine such a scene. In the following script, imagery phrases that can be substituted are in bold, with lake-specific imagery in parentheses.

I would like you to make yourself as comfortable as possible. Keep your eyes closed. Allow yourself to continue relaxing, letting yourself become more and more deeply relaxed. [Pause] *Listen carefully as I describe a peaceful scene.*

*Imagine that you are on a beach **(beside a large, beautiful lake)**. It's a beautiful, warm day and you have decided to go to the **beach (lake)** to catch some sun. The **beach (lake area)** is empty. Bright sunshine bathes the tranquil stretch of **beach (lake)**. As you look up and down the shore, all you can see are miles of clean white sand, **the ebb and flow of gentle waves (the calm and tranquil water of the lake's surface)**, and **tall palm trees (trees surrounding the lake)** lazily blowing in the breeze. The **beach (lake shore)** is nice and warm and sunny and comfortable.*

*As you walk toward the **ocean (lake)**, you can feel the coolness of the sand beneath your bare feet. There is a light breeze blowing today, clean and crisp. And you can smell that special **slightly tangy scent of the ocean (woody scent of the lake)** in the air. You feel **its salty sting on your lips (relaxed)** as the breeze caresses your face.*

When you sit down, you naturally start to wiggle your toes into the cool sand, allowing the sand to slip between your toes. As you dig your toes in the sand, the sun beating down starts to warm the sand and your feet.

You are now lying on your back with your feet stretched out and your arms comfortably beside you. Imagine you are closing your eyes, and pay close attention to the sounds around you. Listen to the sound of **the ebb and flow of the waves, roaring and splashing (the birds chirping overhead and flapping their wings as they fly over the edge of the lake)**, and the soothing sound of the soft blowing wind passing through the trees.

The sun begins to increase the warmth that it radiates. You begin to feel the warmth all over your body. Every now and then, a light breeze gently blows over your body and across your cheeks and face.

You sense the golden glow of the sun through your closed eyes. **You listen carefully to the ocean. In your mind you can see the waves rising, breaking with white foam and then disappearing. . . . As you listen, you can feel your breathing begin to slow and match the pattern of the ocean. (In your mind's eye you slowly open your eyes and things look sort of hazy and far away. The water sparkles and shimmers on the lake's surface. There is a pure blue sky dotted with fluffy white clouds.)** You continue to feel the warmth of the sun and the occasional touch of the cool breeze as it softly blows over your body. You feel very warm and relaxed.

The sounds around you become more and more muffled and begin to fade into the background. You concentrate on the golden glow of the sun and the warmth it makes you feel. **The only sound you can hear is the roar of the ocean: the waves gently surging, then fading away. You can feel your body moving gently with the waves, more and more relaxed. (The quiet calmness of the lake continues to relax you. The only sensation that you experience is the warmth of the sun.)**

As your body reaches an even more relaxed state, your body is fully relaxed, at peace. All your bodily systems have reached a state of balance, of harmony. In this state of balance, resistance to illness may be stronger. Your immune system may work effectively and more efficiently. As you find yourself deeply relaxed, your body is feeling strong and healthy. Notice the feelings of relaxation in your body. Take a few moments to enjoy the sense of balance, peace, and calm.

Now I am going to count backwards from 4 to 1. On the count of 4 start moving your legs; on the count of 3 begin moving your hands and arms; on the count of 2 begin moving your head and neck; and on the count of 1, open your eyes, feeling calm, relaxed, refreshed. 4 . . . 3 . . . 2 . . . 1 . . .

Discussion of Relaxation Exercises (10 minutes)

Ask participants about their experiences with each of the relaxation exercises (breathing, PMR, imagery). Have them describe their thoughts, emotions, and physical sensations during the exercises. Use the following questions:

- "Which exercise did you enjoy the most?"

- "Which exercise did you enjoy the least?"

- "Which aspects of these exercises were particularly easy for you to do?"

- "Which aspects of these exercises were particularly difficult for you to do?"

- "Do you wish to modify these procedures for home use? How so?"

Homework (5 minutes)

Make sure participants have a continued plan for relaxation practice at home. Structuring and planning relaxation practice before participants leave the session may help to ensure compliance. Continue to reinforce relaxation practice; this is critical to participants' success.

✎ Have group members practice PMR for Four Muscle Groups on a daily basis (twice a day if possible). They should record stress levels before and after each practice on the Daily Self-Monitoring Sheet.

✎ Have group members practice diaphragmatic breathing on a daily basis and record stress levels before and after on the Daily Self-Monitoring Sheet.

✎ Have group members perform the imagery exercise at least once a day and record stress levels before and after on the Daily Self-Monitoring Sheet. Participants will find it easiest to practice imagery exercises if they are provided with audio recordings of the scripts used in session.

STRESS MANAGEMENT: *Linking Thoughts and Emotions*

Outline

- Review homework (10 minutes)

- Review the symptoms and effects of stress (5 minutes)

- Explore the relationship between thoughts (appraisals) and feelings (10 minutes)

- Conduct imagery exercise (10 minutes)

- Introduce the appraisal process (10 minutes)

- Assign homework (5 minutes)

- Hand out Session Evaluation Questionnaire (optional) (5 minutes)

Homework Review (10 minutes)

Ask group members whether they are having any difficulty with monitoring their stress levels using the Daily Self-Monitoring Sheet. Review the Thoughts, Feelings, and Physical Sensations Sheet that was assigned last week for homework. Discuss with group members the various stressful situations that they encountered during the week and the corresponding automatic thoughts, emotions, and physical sensations that occurred as a result of these stressors.

Review of the Symptoms and Effects of Stress (5 minutes)

Remind the group that last week members worked to increase awareness of how they are individually affected by stress. This process began with each participant rating various stress-related symptoms according to the degree of personal discomfort that they cause (refer to Symptoms of Stress Checklist in Session 2). Tell the group members that determining individual stress response profiles is an important first step in tailoring the various stress management techniques covered in this program to their individual needs.

These stress-related symptoms were then grouped into five main categories of stress responses that people typically experience. Review these five categories with the group: cognitive, emotional, behavioral, physical, social.

Relationship Between Thoughts (Appraisals) and Feelings (10 minutes)

Having completed last week's exercises, participants should now understand that stress affects each of us in a very specific manner. Unfortunately, many people subscribe to the mistaken belief that stressful situations themselves (rather than their thoughts about these events) are what causes them to feel distress, discomfort, and misery. This week you challenge this notion, suggesting that it is not the actual stressful situations or environmental events that are causing our stress responses, but instead our perceptions and appraisals of these environmental stressors. Explain to the group that the manner in which we process and think about stressful situations when they occur often has a direct impact on our emotions, behavior, and physical well-being. The following example of contrasting perspectives regarding the same issue (HIV infection) can be used to illustrate the point that our thoughts and perceptions of external stressors are what cause our emotions to be moved in either a positive or negative direction.

For example, let us consider the issue of HIV diagnosis. Quite commonly, individuals newly diagnosed with HIV often become extremely upset, believing that they will immediately become sick, that death is just around the corner, and that all future plans are now destroyed.

On the other hand, many individuals living with HIV for long periods of time are much more hopeful about their physical well-being and plans for the future. They believe that with proper diet, exercise, stress management, and medication (if needed) they can remain happy and healthy and continue to pursue life with vigor.

While newly diagnosed individuals experience the same external reality (HIV infection) as individuals diagnosed many years ago, their perceptions and thoughts about their HIV status lead them to have very different emotional responses. In fact, as newly infected individuals obtain more information about HIV disease and solicit social support from other HIV-infected individuals (allowing them to learn more about the realities of their condition), they are more likely to change their perceptions about their illness for the better. They may come to view it more as a manageable condition rather than as an immediate death sentence.

Explore the link between thoughts, emotions, and physical sensations with the group. Have participants complete the Linking Thoughts and Feelings Exercise in the workbook. Discuss the feelings that the participants listed in response to the thoughts/self-talk for each event.

Power of Thought Exercise (10 minutes)

The realization that by changing our thoughts and perceptions we can change how we feel is a critical first step in beginning to manage the distress that we experience in relation to external stressful events. Conduct the following imagery exercise with the group to help demonstrate the power of our thoughts over our emotions and physical sensations.

Ask participants to choose a partner from the group for this exercise. One person takes a few moments to think of three words that mean "weakness" (e.g., weak, fragile, soft). The person then closes his eyes and holds out an arm while repeating those three words over and over. The other partner then puts his hand on the person's arm and tries to pull it down. Partners then reverse roles. Next, each partner repeats the exercise while thinking of words that represent "strength."

Discussion of Imagery Exercise

Ask if participants noticed a difference when repeating words of "strength" rather than words of "weakness." Explain to the group that this exercise illustrates the relationship between the way in which we think and the way that we feel both emotionally and physically. Thinking about words associated with strength made participants' arms feel stronger; conversely, imagining words representing weakness made their limbs feel tired and limp. You can use the following dialogue to summarize:

> *Remember that no external stimulus was present during this exercise; it was simply the power of your thoughts and images that created the physical sensations. Now imagine how your body must react if you think anxious and depressing thoughts during the day. Your muscles may feel tired and tense, you may feel sad, and your body may be quite agitated, along with a host of other symptoms that simply arise from the negative and fearful thoughts that you are thinking.*

Tell group members that your goal is to help them identify the stressful situations that they encounter in their environment, the negative thoughts associated with these events, and the unpleasant emotions, behaviors, and physical sensations associated with these negative thoughts. At this point, you might encourage group members to share one or two stressful experiences from the previous week, and also identify any negative thoughts, emotions, or physical sensations that resulted from these experiences. This kind of sharing promotes group process and allows participants to begin personalizing the information provided during the session.

The Appraisal Process (10 minutes)

The next step is to identify those negative thoughts that are excessive and unrealistic (as opposed to those negative thoughts that are valid and realistic perceptions of a stressful situation). Participants can then begin the process of modifying and changing these thoughts to more realistic and accurate perceptions, which will likely produce considerable reductions in distress levels. In order to understand the origins of our negative thinking, we need to know how we appraise (or interpret) stressful events.

The appraisal process includes several components:

- Recognition that a relationship exists between what you think and how you feel

- Awareness of how your perceptions and appraisals of external events are contributing to your moods and emotions

- Identification of the accuracy of your perceptions and appraisals of external events, which are sometimes accurate and sometimes inaccurate

Before we really experience an event we must process it and give it meaning. We must think about what is happening and understand it before really feeling it. If our perceptions about an external event are correct and accurate, then our emotions and mood will be appropriate and match the situation. Accurate negative thinking can help us process the situation and take appropriate action. (Refer to the examples given in the section of the workbook entitled "Beneficial Aspects of Negative Thinking.") Conversely, if our perceptions or thoughts inaccurately reflect the external reality, then our feelings may also become distorted, extreme, and unreasonably negative. Erroneous thoughts often contribute to unpleasant emotions and symptoms of physical distress.

Distressing and upsetting emotions often signal that we are engaging in some form of negative thinking. By examining our negative thoughts during these troubling emotional states, we can distinguish between accurate negative thoughts and those that arise from inaccurate perceptions of external stressful events. We can then attempt to modify and change those distorted thought processes that are causing us unnecessary distress. The following story illustrates this process.

An individual who lost his job and was seeking new employment found himself quite anxious and depressed before a job interview. He examined his negative thoughts—"I will never get this job; I am not qualified; the people here will never like me"—and found that it was likely he was appraising the situation in an overly negative and unrealistic manner. Thus, he attempted to break his cycle of negative emotion by changing his negative thoughts to something more positive, like, "I have an even chance of getting this job; I am well prepared for this interview; if I don't get this job, there are several other jobs adver-

tised for which I am qualified." These more realistic and accurate
thoughts reduced his anxiety and depression levels and helped him to
feel more comfortable in the interview.

Steps of the Appraisal Process

Explain to the group that while this technique is simple enough, it does take a lot of practice to use it effectively. Several steps are involved.

Step 1: Become Aware of Negative Thinking Patterns

In the preceding example, the interviewee first had to become aware that he was saying something unrealistically negative to himself.

Step 2: Learn to Recognize Anxiety-Producing Appraisals

Next he had to learn to recognize his anxiety-producing appraisals (thoughts about the situation). Negative thoughts like "I am not qualified" were making him feel depressed and anxious.

Step 3: Begin to Notice That These Thoughts Are Automatic

Thoughts like the ones the interviewee had occur so quickly that we refer to them as "automatic." His judgment that "people here will never like me" is not based on an assessment of the situation but on habitual assumptions.

Step 4: Take Note That These Thoughts Are Often Negative and Distorted

The automatic thoughts that are associated with anxiety and other negative emotions are often negative and distorted. For example, the thought "I'll never get this job" is an unrealistic appraisal of the situation, because the employer was impressed enough with the man's résumé to call him for an interview. The employer was willing to consider giving him the job, so he did in fact have some chance.

Step 5: Begin to Change to More Balanced Appraisals

Once the interviewee learned to identify his negative thoughts, he could then work on changing them. With practice, less distorted thoughts (i.e., more balanced appraisals) would become automatic, and the process of identifying and changing unrealistic negative thoughts would also become automatic.

Homework (5 minutes)

✎ Have group members continue to monitor their stress levels at specified times each day and record on the Daily Self-Monitoring Sheet.

✎ Have group members review the Linking Thoughts and Feelings Exercise in the workbook.

✎ Have group members complete a copy of the Thoughts, Feelings, and Physical Sensations Monitoring Sheet from Session 2. They may want to select one stressful event per day to focus their attention on for about 20 minutes.

Session Evaluation (optional) (5 minutes)

See example of Session Evaluation Questionnaire at the end of chapter 3.

Chapter 6

Session 4: Breathing, Imagery, Passive Progressive Muscle Relaxation / Negative Thinking and Cognitive Distortions

(Corresponds to chapter 5 of the workbook)

Materials Needed

- ▨ PMR script from Session 1

- ▨ Relaxation mats

- ▨ Flip chart or blackboard

- ▨ Copy of the participant workbook

- ▨ Copies of audio recording of Diaphragmatic Breathing with Imagery script (optional)

- ▨ Copies of audio recording of PMR with Imagery script (optional)

- ▨ Copies of Stress Responses and Types of Negative Thoughts Monitoring Sheet (optional)

- ▨ Copies of Daily Self-Monitoring Sheet (optional)

- ▨ Copies of Session Evaluation Questionnaire (optional)

RELAXATION TRAINING: *Breathing, Imagery, Passive Progressive Muscle Relaxation*

Outline

■ Discuss home relaxation practice (5 minutes)

■ Review diaphragmatic breathing (5 minutes)

■ Combine diaphragmatic breathing with imagery (10 minutes)

■ Conduct passive PMR with special place imagery (35 minutes)

■ Assign homework (5 minutes)

Discussion of Home Relaxation Practice (5 minutes)

Determine what facilitates doing exercises at home or at work. Identify what interferes with practice. Review participants' Daily Self-Monitoring Sheets for adherence. Ask group members:

■ "How often do you find you are relaxing?"

■ "Where are you practicing relaxation?"

■ "What gets in the way for you?"

■ "Do you find yourself encountering obstacles to doing relaxation?"

■ "What do you say to yourself that keeps you from taking the time to practice relaxation?"

■ "What have you done or said to help keep your commitment to relax?"

Diaphragmatic Breathing Review (5 minutes)

Do a quick review of diaphragmatic breathing with the group. Have participants breathe in to the count of 4, hold to the count of 4, exhale to the count of 4, and hold to the count of 4.

Breathe in, 1 . . . , 2 . . . , 3 . . . , 4 . . . Hold, 1 . . . , 2 . . . , 3 . . . , 4 . . .
Breathe out, 1 . . . , 2 . . . , 3 . . . , 4 . . . Hold, 1 . . . , 2 . . . , 3 . . . , 4 . . .
[Repeat several times.]

Remind participants that they can use this kind of breathing to calm down in any situation, without anyone even noticing.

Diaphragmatic Breathing with Imagery (10 minutes)

This exercise combines the relaxing benefits of deep relaxed breathing with self-suggestions.

Lie down on your mat in a relaxed position. Place your hands gently on your abdomen and continue deep breathing to the count of 4. Imagine that with each breath of air coming in, energy is coming into your lungs. As you hold, energy is being stored in the center of your body and flowing out to all parts of your body. Imagine that as you exhale, any tension is leaving your body. Form a picture of this in your mind, breathing in and letting energy come into your body, holding, and letting the energy flow through your body. Breathe out, letting go of any tension, and hold, letting yourself remain in a clear, calm, state. [Participants continue to breathe quietly for a few minutes.] *Gradually bring yourself back to the room and open your eyes.*

Discuss how the exercise went. Ask group members how relaxed they were able to become. Have them compare it to PMR for achieving relaxation.

Passive PMR with Special Place Imagery (35 minutes)

With this exercise, participants recall the relaxation of doing PMR using four muscle groups while imagining a safe, secure place. Review the procedure for PMR and have group members tense and relax the four muscle groups used during last week's PMR session (i.e., stomach, chest, shoulders, forehead). This review reminds participants of the difference between the feelings of relaxation and those of tension. Explain to participants that from this point on, they will no longer actually tense the muscles but instead will simply remember what that tension felt like.

In conducting Passive PMR for Four Muscle Groups, you will follow the exact script used during last week's four-muscle-group PMR session. However, remind participants that when you tell them to tense the various muscle groups (you will read the script for these four muscle groups from Session 1 verbatim), they are *not* to tense the muscles but instead simply remember what that tension felt like and then continue to relax the muscles as instructed.

Next instruct group members in the use of special place imagery. Begin by having them think of a special place—a place they have been or have seen in a movie or a picture, or an imaginary place—where they feel calm and safe. When they have selected a place, they are ready to begin the relaxation experience. You may want to tell participants that they may change the place if they want during the exercise. Explain that the Special Place Imagery exercise is a deep passive relaxation experience in which participants combine the images of their previously selected special place with the images you suggest to create a calming effect.

To conduct this relaxation exercise, first take participants through Passive PMR for Four Muscle Groups (using the instructions provided in the beginning of this section), and then without stopping move immediately into the Special Place Imagery exercise (using the following script). This allows group members to gain the benefits of both procedures during the same relaxation session.

Special Place Imagery Script

Allow yourself to become comfortable and gently focus on your breathing. Notice how you can achieve a rhythm of breathing, deeper and deeper, slower and slower, becoming more and more relaxed with every breath. Just allow yourself to slow down. Slowly, gently, calmly, breathe in and out.

As you breathe in you can mentally say to yourself a word like "relax" or any phrase that will help you just let go and bring yourself to a deeper state of calm and peace.

As you breathe out, you can let go of all your tension, all your stress—just let it go and let it leave your body. With every exhalation, let the tension go, allowing yourself to become more and more relaxed.

Focus on your breath gently, quietly. Watch the breathing in and out. If you notice thoughts going by, it's okay. Just notice them as they drift by. As you continue to breathe slowly and deeply, you may notice feelings of comfort and warmth.

Allow yourself to breathe in the comfort and calm your body experiences in a relaxed state. As you are feeling completely relaxed, imagine a place, a special place that you enjoy, where you feel peaceful, calm, and relaxed. It may be a place where you feel secure and safe, or where you have experienced a sense of beauty, joy, or awe.

Imagine yourself going to your special place now in your mind. Let yourself be in that place now. Breathe deeply and feel its peace. Feel that place begin to fill you with a deep sense of calm and joy. Look around you. See the shapes and colors of your special place. Can you see the sun? What are the textures that you see? What do you hear? Smell the air. Can you feel its freshness? What is the temperature? Can you feel the sun on your skin? Do you feel a cool breeze against your face? Be aware of all the sensations in your special place. Feel the peace of your special place.

Breathe in, and as you breathe in, let yourself be completely filled with the serenity of this special place. Allow yourself to experience its beauty. Let it nourish and calm you. Go over these different sensations again, allowing yourself to become more and more relaxed. With every breath, let the calmness spread deeper through your body, restoring every cell, bringing energy, healing, relaxing wholeness throughout your body.

[Pause for 1 minute.]

Breathe in the calm deeper and deeper, letting it fill you. Know that this is a place you always have inside of you, and that you have the ability to go there any time you want by breathing deeply in and out, gently closing your eyes, and taking yourself to this inner healing place.

Now, I am going to count backward from 4 to 1. When I say 4, you can begin to move your feet and toes. When I say 3, you can begin to move your arms and hands. When I count to 2, you can begin to move your head and neck. And on 1, you can stretch and gradually open your eyes, coming to a fully alert state, but retaining the calm and peace of this relaxation experience. 4 . . . 3 . . . 2 . . . 1 . . .

Discussion

- "What was this experience like for you?"

- "How did this compare to what you have done previously?"

- "What was the memory of tensing and relaxing like as compared to actually tensing and relaxing?"

- "Did anyone have more trouble concentrating?"

- "Were you able to find your relaxed place? What was it like there?"

If participants had trouble using imagery or finding a relaxed place, you may explain that visualization can be initially difficult for some people. Conducting short visualization exercises with group members who experienced difficulty with imagery can be useful. By practicing simpler exercises first, they will be better able to tackle the more complex imagery scenes used in later relaxation sessions. Explain that with continued practice, these exercises will become easier and easier.

Homework (5 minutes)

✎ Have group members practice diaphragmatic breathing with imagery on a daily basis (twice a day if possible). They should record stress levels before and after each practice on the Daily Self-Monitoring Sheet.

✎ Have group members practice passive PMR with special place imagery on a daily basis (twice a day if possible). They should record stress levels before and after each practice on the Daily Self-Monitoring Sheet.

Negative Thinking and Cognitive Distortions

Outline

- Review homework (10 minutes)

- Examine negative thinking and cognitive distortions (20 minutes)

- Discuss the effect of negative thinking on behavior (10 minutes)

- Practice identifying negative thoughts (20 minutes)

- Assign homework (5 minutes)

- Hand out Session Evaluation Questionnaire (optional) (5 minutes)

Homework Review (10 minutes)

Ask group members whether they are having any difficulty with monitoring their stress levels using the Daily Self-Monitoring Sheets. Review the Thoughts, Feelings, and Physical Sensations Monitoring Sheet assigned as homework last week.

Discuss with group members the various stressful situations that they encountered during the week. Focus on the distorted negative thoughts that resulted from these situations and the corresponding emotions and physical sensations.

Negative Thinking and Cognitive Distortions (20 minutes)

Last session included an examination of how thoughts, emotions, and physical sensations are all interrelated. Now you will discuss with the group how distorted negative thoughts arising from inaccurate appraisals of stressful situations often contribute to negative mood states (e.g., depression or anxiety), unpleasant emotions (e.g., sadness or guilt), and uncomfortable physical states (e.g., muscle tension or headaches). Remind group members, however, that negative thoughts do not always represent inaccurate or distorted views of reality. Sometimes our perceptions and appraisals about stressors are accurate, and in these cases, our emotions (even unpleasant ones) will likely be accurate as well and useful to our adaptation. It is only when our appraisals are distorted or inaccurate that our emotional reactions will be extreme and cause us unnecessary distress. One of the goals of this program is to help participants distinguish between accurate and distorted negative thoughts, and subsequently to help them to restructure distorted negative thoughts into more rational, realistic, and positive thoughts that decrease distress.

This session's focus is on the negative thinking patterns and cognitive distortions that people typically use. More specifically, the group will examine the cognitive distortions that each member utilizes most often, the situations that trigger these distortions, and the negative emotions and physical sensations that arise as a result of these distortions. Have participants refer to the section in the workbook entitled "Examples of Negative Thinking and Cognitive Distortions." These pages cover the same cognitive distortions that are listed here, except in more detail.

Have group members take turns reading the workbook descriptions of cognitive distortions. After reading a description, encourage each group member to generate an example from her own life when she has used that distortion. This helps facilitate group discussion and allows group members to better understand the ways in which other people's emotional states are affected by negative thought processes.

Examples of Negative Thinking and Cognitive Distortions (Adapted from Burns, 1981)

1. *All-or-Nothing Thinking:* You think in black-and-white terms: "You're either for me or against me."

2. *Overgeneralization:* You assume that one situation in your life applies to all others: "This relationship didn't work; nobody will ever want me."

3. *Mental Filter:* You filter out anything positive so that everything seems negative: "They think I am a total idiot."

4. *Disqualifying the Positive:* You insist that positive experiences and communications from others such as compliments don't count: "They are just being nice to me."

5. *Jumping to Conclusions:* You make a negative interpretation in the absence of definite facts to convincingly support your conclusion. There are two types of this: "mind reading" and the "fortune teller error."

    a. *Mind reading:* You assume that you know what others think: "He didn't say hi to me, so he must not like me anymore."

    b. *Fortune teller error:* You think you can forecast the distant future: "I am HIV-infected; therefore, I have nothing but heartache to look forward to."

6. *Magnification (Catastrophizing) or Minimization:* You either magnify the importance of things, as if you were looking through binoculars that make them look larger then they really are, or you minimize the significance of things, as if you were looking through the wrong end of the binoculars. Magnification is seen in this thought: "I have the sniffles; it must be PCP (Pneumocystis pneumonia)." An example of minimization is, "I worked hard on that project, but it's not a big deal."

7. *Emotional Reasoning:* You believe that your feelings are an accurate reflection of reality: "I feel depressed; therefore, I'm a loser."

8. *"Should" Statements:* You use words that reflect a rigid view of the world and the world's expectations of your behavior: "I should have prepared my presentation better."

9. *Labeling and Mislabeling:* You assign personal traits to single episodes of a behavior: "I messed up this project; I'm stupid."

10. *Personalization:* You assume responsibility for events that may not be entirely under your control: "My lover is depressed, and it's my fault."

After reviewing the entire list, have group members discuss their favorite negative thoughts. Determine which negative thoughts they identified with the most.

Also, ask each member to think about a specific situation where she was anxious or depressed. Have each identify any examples of negative thinking used in that situation. You should give your own examples in order to get the ball rolling (see the Labeling Cognitive Distortions and Corresponding Emotions Exercise in the workbook).

Negative Thoughts and Behaviors (10 minutes)

Explain to the group that negative thoughts and cognitive distortions not only contribute to unpleasant emotions and physical states but may also negatively affect one's behavior in several ways. You may want to use the following examples in your discussion:

- If you think that you no one can love you anymore based on one negative relationship (overgeneralization), you may withdraw from people and miss the opportunity to meet someone new

- If you think that the situation is the worst thing that could happen (catastrophizing), you may give up attempts at staying healthy and take up drinking, smoking, or drug use to deal with painful emotions

- If you think that you can't do anything to improve the situation (all-or-nothing thinking), you may simply deny that problems exist to avoid dealing with them

Explain to the group that chronic use of these kind of behaviors often causes the problems to grow bigger, creating more stress and leading the person to engage in even more negative thinking and cognitive distortions. Emphasize that identifying negative thought patterns is the first step in breaking this vicious cycle of thoughts, behaviors, and stress.

Identifying Negative Thoughts Exercise (20 minutes)

Have group members select one of the stressful situations previously identified in their homework (Thoughts, Feelings, and Physical Sensations Monitoring Sheet). Have them discuss the different types of negative thoughts that they engaged in during these situations. Encourage them to make connections between their negative thoughts and their behavior.

Homework (5 minutes)

✎ Have group members continue to monitor their stress levels at specified times each day and record on the Daily Self-Monitoring Sheet.

✎ Have group members complete the Labeling Cognitive Distortions and Corresponding Emotions Exercise in the workbook.

✎ Have group members complete the Stress Responses and Types of Negative Thoughts Monitoring Sheet to identify the types of negative thinking associated with their stressful situations this week.

Session Evaluation (optional) (5 minutes)

See example of Session Evaluation Questionnaire at the end of chapter 3.

Chapter 7

Session 5: Autogenic Training for Heaviness and Warmth / Rational Thought Replacement

---

(Corresponds to chapter 6 of the workbook)

Materials Needed

- PMR script from Session 1

- Relaxation mats

- Flip chart or blackboard

- Copy of the participant workbook

- Copies of audio recording of Autogenic script for Heaviness and Warmth (optional)

- Copies of Rational Thought Replacement Sheet (optional)

- Copies of Stress Responses and Types of Negative Thoughts Monitoring Sheet (optional)

- Copies of Daily Self-Monitoring Sheet (optional)

- Copies of Session Evaluation Questionnaire (optional)

RELAXATION TRAINING: *Autogenic Training for Heaviness and Warmth*

Outline

- Discuss home relaxation practice (5 minutes)

- Discuss integration of relaxation with stress management (5 minutes)

- Review diaphragmatic breathing (5 minutes)

- Review passive PMR (15 minutes)

- Introduce autogenic training (10 minutes)

- Give instructions for autogenic training (10 minutes)

- Conduct heaviness and warmth autogenic exercise (10 minutes)

- Assign homework (5 minutes)

Discussion of Home Relaxation Practice (5 minutes)

Determine what facilitates doing exercises at home or at work. Identify what interferes with practice. Review participants' Daily Self-Monitoring Sheets for adherence. Ask group members:

- "How often do you find you are relaxing?"

- "Where are you practicing relaxation?"

- "What gets in the way for you?"

- "Do you find yourself encountering obstacles to doing relaxation?"

- "What do you say to yourself that keeps you from taking the time to practice relaxation?"

- "What have you done or said to help keep your commitment to relax?"

Integration of Relaxation with Stress Management (5 minutes)

Discuss with the group how relaxation helps with stress management. Prompt for how doing relaxation exercises on a regular basis can make them more aware of how they hold tension and whether they are experiencing negative emotions. Relaxation can also help them be more open to creative alternatives for replacing distorted thoughts. Questions to ask include:

- "To what degree do relaxation exercises help you become more aware of hidden tensions in your body?"

- "Are the relaxation and breathing exercises making you more aware of your anxious thoughts and fears?"

- "To what extent does being able to relax give you time to come up with alternative strategies for dealing with problems?"

Explain that relaxation can be employed for several purposes:

Prevention

Relaxation can be used in anticipation of a tension-arousing situation. It may prevent you from becoming anxious and distracted.

Preparation

Relaxation can help carry out a challenging cognitive or behavioral coping response. It can prepare you to deal with problems or handle long-term stressors by giving you the mental energy to be flexible and creative in using different strategies.

Recovering

Relaxation can be used to return to baseline once an overwhelming situation has occurred. It can help you get back on track after you have resolved the situation.

Diaphragmatic Breathing Review (5 minutes)

Do a quick review of diaphragmatic breathing with the group. Have participants breathe in to the count of 4, hold to the count of 4, exhale to the count of 4, and hold to the count of 4.

Breathe in, 1 . . . , 2 . . . , 3 . . . , 4 . . . Hold, 1 . . . , 2 . . . , 3 . . . , 4 . . .
Breathe out, 1 . . . , 2 . . . , 3 . . . , 4 . . . Hold, 1 . . . , 2 . . . , 3 . . . , 4 . . .
[Repeat several times.]

Remind participants that they can use this kind of breathing to calm down in any situation, without anyone even noticing.

Passive PMR Review (15 minutes)

Take group members through the same Passive PMR for Four Muscle Groups exercise practiced last session. This is accomplished by using the PMR script for the four muscle groups from Session 1 and the instructions for Passive PMR from Session 4. Remind participants that they will not be tensing the muscle groups but simply remembering what the sensations of tension felt like.

Introduction of Autogenic Training (10 minutes)

Autogenic training is a powerful and well-researched method of relaxation based on the research of Oskar Vogt and Johannes Schultz, two physicians living in Berlin around the turn of the 20th century. Vogt found that he was able to teach individuals to induce a state of deep relaxation in themselves with auto(self)-suggestions. Schultz found that self-suggestions inducing heaviness and warmth could also induce a state of deep relaxation very similar to a hypnotic trance. Applying his knowledge of yoga, hypnosis, and self-suggestion, Schultz developed the autogenic method for people wishing to achieve deep relaxation through self-suggestion without reliance on a hypnotist.

Autogenic training includes six standard exercises to be done in a specific sequence. These exercises deal with helping the body to relax and restoring a state of balance following the "fight-or-flight" stress response. Advanced exercises are designed to help focus the mind and to address specific problems. Exercises involve focusing attention on specific parts of the body, repeating specific phrases, and then passively allowing the body to respond, rather than forcing any particular desired response. The first standard exercise uses the theme of heaviness. As part of the stress response, tension is increased in the striated voluntary muscles to enable an individual to either "fight" or "flee from" a potential threat. The blood vessels in the limbs also constrict during the stress response. The suggestion to induce heaviness in the limbs is designed to counteract the stress-related contraction in the voluntary muscles of the arms and legs, and to allow these muscles to relax. The second exercise is designed to promote vasodilation in the peripheral blood vessels, thus enabling warmth to spread in the limbs. The third exercise directs the attention to balancing cardiac activity. The fourth exercise allows breathing to become regular and natural, the fifth exercise relaxes the abdomen, and the sixth exercise relaxes the muscles of the face and forehead.

Autogenic training has been used successfully as a treatment for a variety of disorders, including hypertension, headaches, diabetes, low back pain, asthma, sleep disorders, arthritis, cold extremities, and thyroid problems. It has also been helpful for emotional and mental problems such as anxiety, irritability, and fatigue. Because autogenic training is powerful enough to produce changes in physiological measures such as blood pressure, skin temperature, blood sugar, and hormone secretions, it must be used carefully. For instance, a sudden change in blood pressure during an exercise could lead to fainting.

Instructions for Autogenic Training (10 minutes)

Before beginning the actual autogenic exercise, instruct participants on the procedure to be used. You may want to use the following dialogue in your instructions:

> *Autogenic training involves repeating simple verbal phrases or formulas, such as, "My right arm is heavy . . . My right arm is warm." When you repeat a formula, say it slowly, concentrating on the part of the body you are describing, and then pause for a few seconds when you are finished. Each formula should be repeated three times. If you are right-handed, start with your right arm and then proceed to your left arm. If you are left-handed, do the opposite.*

Review the body parts to be used:

1. Arms

2. Legs

3. Neck and shoulders

Explain that for the first autogenic exercise they will be practicing inducing heaviness and then warmth in each body part. This is done by repeating the simple formulas, "My _____ is heavy" and "My _____ is warm." (See following autogenic script.)

Imagery

For those participants who have difficulty feeling a sense of heaviness, visual imagery can be used to supplement the verbal formulas. For example, a visual image of weights or bags of sand attached to the arms and legs might augment the feeling of heaviness. For warmth, imagining lying on a beach with the sun pouring over the body or imagining blood vessels opening up and warm blood flowing out to the fingertips and toes may increase the sensation of warmth.

Passive Concentration

Tell group members that as they do these exercises, they should allow themselves to experience whatever feelings and sensations come without judgment or expectations. They should be aware of their physical sensations but should not analyze them or try to force them in any particular direction. This observant attitude is often called passive concentration or "witnessing." To illustrate, say that passive concentration is like the attention we use when we watch a movie: we just watch what's on the screen. Unlike meditation, which is covered later in the program, autogenics concentrates on physical sensations rather than mental states.

Preparation for Practice

Tell group members that when they first practice autogenics, it is best to minimize all outside noises and distractions. They should practice relaxation somewhere they will not be disturbed. After they are skilled at achieving a state of relaxation, it will be easier to practice relaxation in a setting such as the workplace or in an unfamiliar location. As they become skilled, they can practice autogenic exercises for a few minutes—for example, while waiting for a phone call or for an elevator—as well as for longer time periods.

This program's autogenic training progresses at a more rapid pace than is traditionally used. In standard autogenic training, exercises are taught very slowly, so that it may take several weeks to complete training for feeling warmth in both arms and legs and as much as 4 to 10 months to master the entire set of six exercises. Since this program completes autogenic training in only four sessions, emphasize to participants the importance of regular daily practice. Recommend to participants that they practice twice a day. These exercises are best done before meals—for example, in the afternoon before dinner, or in the morning before breakfast.

For practice, the temperature should be kept at a comfortable level. Instruct participants to wear comfortable clothing and loosen restrictive attire (take off belts, shoes, jewelry, etc.).

Group members can do the exercises sitting or lying down. They should keep their heads supported, legs about eight inches apart, toes pointed slightly outward, and arms resting comfortably at their sides without touching them.

Explain to the participants that if they feel increased anxiety or restlessness during or after the exercises, or experience disturbing side effects such as lightheadedness from decreased blood pressure, they should go back to practicing progressive muscle relaxation exercises instead.

Heaviness and Warmth Autogenic Exercise (10 minutes)

Get into a comfortable position. Close your eyes. Inhale and exhale slowly and deeply. Let go of the events of the day and allow your mind to empty. If thoughts or feelings come up, just notice them and let them pass by as if you were watching them on a movie screen.

Begin by saying to yourself, "I am completely relaxed and at peace." Repeat this phrase slowly three times while breathing deeply, releasing tension with every exhale.

Focus on your right arm and feel it becoming heavy. Say to yourself three times, "My right arm is heavy." Pause between each repetition of the phrase and concentrate on the feeling of heaviness. Then move your attention to your left arm and say to yourself three times, "My left arm is heavy." Feel your arm becoming heavier with each repetition of the phrase. Concentrate on the heaviness in both your arms and say to yourself three times, "Both of my arms are heavy." Breathe deeply and feel yourself becoming more re-laxed with every exhale.

Repeat the preceding instructions, substituting legs for arms. Then continue with the following:

Now feel the heaviness in both your arms and legs. Say to yourself three times, "My arms and legs are heavy." Continue to breathe slowly and deeply. Turn your attention to your neck and shoulders; say to yourself three times, "My neck and shoulders are heavy." Feel yourself becoming heavier and heavier, more and more relaxed with each exhale of the breath.

Repeat the entire preceding sequence, substituting "warmth" for "heaviness." End the session with:

Now rest for a few minutes as you gradually become more alert. Say to yourself three times, "I am relaxed and alert." Inhale deeply and exhale, letting go of any remaining tension. When you are ready, slowly open your eyes.

Discussion of Autogenic Experience

- "To what extent did you feel heaviness or warmth?"

- "Were you able to just watch your experiences with an attitude of passive concentration?"

- "Was it easier to feel heaviness or warmth in some places as opposed to others?"

- "How did the sense of relaxation compare to PMR?"

- "Did you have any disturbing sensations?"

Homework (5 minutes)

Have group members practice any of the types of relaxation taught so far in the program (i.e., PMR, breathing, imagery, autogenic training).

The only guideline is that participants practice twice a day and record stress levels before and after on the Daily Self-Monitoring Sheet.

STRESS MANAGEMENT: *Rational Thought Replacement*

Outline

- Review homework (10 minutes)

- Discuss differences between irrational and rational self-talk (25 minutes)

- Introduce steps to rational thought replacement (15 minutes)

- Practice rational thought replacement (10 minutes)

- Assign homework (5 minutes)

- Hand out Session Evaluation Questionnaire (optional) (5 minutes)

Homework Review (10 minutes)

Give each group member the opportunity to describe stressful situations and one of the self-talk scenarios from the Stress Responses and Types of Negative Thoughts Monitoring Sheet. Examine the different types of negative thinking that are brought up.

Differences Between Irrational and Rational Self-Talk (25 minutes)

As discussed in the last session, the thoughts that we have in response to stressful situations may reflect whether we have perceived a situation accurately or inaccurately. When we appraise a situation correctly, our thoughts are generally realistic and appropriate for the situation. *Rational self-talk* reflects appropriate concern for the difficulties that we face, demonstrating a balanced perception of reality. For example, "This is a difficult situation, but there are things I can do to improve it."

In contrast, inaccurate perceptions of stressful situations often lead us to either deny that problems exist or blow the magnitude of problems far out of proportion. *Irrational self-talk* often keeps us from dealing directly with our problems, causing them to build until they are out of control. Examples of irrational self-talk are, "It's not really a problem. I'll just ignore it" or "This is a catastrophe! There's nothing I can do to fix it."

This last example clearly depicts the process of distorted negative thinking. Cognitive distortions often cause us to feel significant emotional and physical distress that can be alleviated only by changing negative thinking patterns. The goal for this session is to take participants' distorted thoughts and restructure them so that they reflect accurate perceptions of reality while still showing appropriate concern over the stressors.

Identifying Irrational and Rational Self-Talk Exercise

In the following exercise, participants practice identifying rational and irrational thinking as it arises in various stressful situations. This will help them to later identify such thinking patterns in themselves.

Part 1

Have group members imagine a scene where an individual is being fired from his job. Have participants role-play a later scene when the person is sitting at home thinking about the reasons why he was fired. Have different group members role-play examples of irrational and rational thinking (speaking their thoughts out loud) that might occur in such an individual due to his termination.

Part 2

Have the participants complete the Identifying Irrational and Rational Self-Talk Exercise in the workbook.

Steps to Rational Thought Replacement (15 minutes)

The group has now spent a considerable amount of time both this session and last examining the make-up of negative thought patterns, especially those patterns that reflect cognitive distortions. Remind the group that a major component of stress management involves increasing awareness of distorted thought patterns, identifying how these thoughts contribute to various states of emotional and physical distress, and then changing (or restructuring) these negative thought processes so that they are more in line with reality. Emphasize to participants that in changing their distorted negative thoughts (remember that some negative thoughts are accurate perceptions of reality) they are likely to improve their emotional and physical well-being.

Review the following five steps (A, B, C, D, E) to refuting and replacing inaccurate or negative self-talk (adapted from Burns, 1981).

Step A: Become AWARE: Identify Self-Talk

Participants must first become aware of their automatic thoughts. They can then identify those that are negative and possibly inaccurate. They should also identify the feelings and behaviors related to their self-talk.

Step B: Rate Your BELIEF in Each Negative Thought

Participants select a negative thought and rate the extent to which they believed that thought was true at the time when they were thinking it. If they were completely convinced that the thought was true, they would rate it 100%. If they believed that there was no truth to the thought, then they would rate it 0%.

Step C: CHALLENGE Yourself: Dispute Negative Self-Talk

Participants select a negative thought (perhaps from their homework) and challenge their thinking with the following questions:

- "What actual support is there for this idea?"

- "What evidence exists that this idea is false?"

- "What is the worst thing that could happen to me?"

  - "How bad is that worst thing?"

  - "How likely is that outcome?"

  - "How could I handle the worst case scenario?"

- "What good things might occur? How likely are they to happen?"

Step D: DISCARD the Distortion: Change the Negative Thought to a More Rational One

Participants can use the following questions to help them discard negative thoughts and replace them with rational responses:

- "What can I say to myself that will reduce excessive negative feelings?"

- "What can I say to myself that will be self-enhancing, instead of a put-down?"

- "What can I say to myself that will help me cope with the situation appropriately?"

- "How do I want to feel and act in this situation?"

- "What do I need to say to myself that will help bring that about?"

Participants then rate their belief in their rational responses on a scale of 0% to 100%.

Step E: EVALUATE the Outcome

The last step is to evaluate the outcome of changing negative thinking. First, participants re-rate their belief in their automatic negative thoughts on a scale of 0% to 100%. Then they specify and rate (0% to 100%) the emotions associated with those thoughts.

Rational Thought Replacement Exercise (10 minutes)

Have the group practice using Steps A through E for the following situations and corresponding thoughts. For this exercise, participants can use the Rational Thought Replacement Sheet. You may photocopy this form from the workbook or download multiple copies from the Treatments *ThatWork*™ Web site at www.oup.com/us/ttw.

Situation 1: Your lover has just broken up with you.

Thoughts: "I'll never have a lover again." "I'll always be alone." "I am a failure at relationships."

Situation 2: You get a cold with a cough.

Thoughts: "I must have PCP." "This is going to be the end." "The worst will always happen to me."

Next have group members describe a stressful situation from their homework. Have them use the Rational Thought Replacement Sheet to go through the five steps (A through E) of rational thought replacement.

Discussion

Discuss the rational thought replacement process with the group using the following questions:

■ "Do alternative responses sometimes feel unnatural?"

■ "How does a rational response become an automatic thought?"

Explain that it is normal for replacing thoughts to feel unnatural since they are trying to gain control over a process that has previously operated in an automatic fashion. By practicing Steps A through E , they will become more used to intercepting distorted automatic thoughts and replacing them with more rational alternatives. However, they may find that this replacement process will never quite be automatic and will require a conscious effort on their part.

Generating Rational Responses

Probably the most difficult aspect of rational thought replacement for many people involves generating rational responses that are genuine and believable. If participants find it difficult to generate rational responses, have them try using the following examples as an initial response to inaccurate self-talk. These examples can be expanded upon by creating additional rational thoughts appropriate for the situation.

- "I may feel a negative emotion, but the situation itself doesn't do anything to me"

- "Nobody's perfect"

- "It takes two to have a conflict"

- "We can influence how we feel by the way we think"

Helpful Guidelines for Generating Rational Responses

- Pick specific thoughts to refute and replace

- Deal with specific problems, not with general philosophical stances

- If you get stuck and can't think of a rational response, come back to it

- Think of how someone else would respond

- Think of how you would respond to someone else in the same situation

- Ask someone else how he or she would respond

- Identify flag words in your thinking such as "always," "never," "should," "can't"

- Learn to describe events in less extreme terms: use terms such as "inconvenient," "disappointing," "frustrating," or "well-done," as opposed to "terrible," "horrible," "catastrophic," or "perfect"

Homework (5 minutes)

✎ Have group members continue to monitor their stress levels at specified times each day and record on the Daily Self-Monitoring Sheet.

✎ Have group members review the Identifying Irrational and Rational Self-Talk Exercise in the workbook.

✎ Have group members continue to use the Stress Responses and Types of Negative Thoughts Monitoring Sheet (from Session 4).

✎ Have group members complete Rational Thought Replacement Sheets for three separate stressful situations.

✎ Have group members complete the Situations This Week that I Will Have to Cope With worksheet in the workbook.

Session Evaluation (optional) (5 minutes)

See example of Session Evaluation Questionnaire at the end of chapter 3.

Chapter 8

Session 6: Autogenic Training for Heartbeat, Breathing, Abdomen, and Forehead / Productive Coping

(Corresponds to chapter 7 of the workbook)

Materials Needed

- Autogenic script from Session 5

- Relaxation mats

- Flip chart or blackboard

- Copy of the participant workbook

- Copies of audio recording of Autogenic script for Heaviness, Warmth, Heartbeat, Breathing, Abdomen, and Forehead (optional)

- Copies of Coping Response Monitoring Sheet (optional)

- Copies of Daily Self-Monitoring Sheet (optional)

- Copies of Session Evaluation Questionnaire (optional)

RELAXATION TRAINING: *Autogenic Training for Heartbeat, Breathing, Abdomen, and Forehead*

Outline

- Discuss home relaxation practice (5 minutes)

- Review diaphragmatic breathing (5 minutes)

- Conduct autogenic training (30 minutes)

- Assign homework (five minutes)

Discussion of Home Relaxation Practice (5 minutes)

Determine and address any difficulties participants have had with practice during the week, or with any symptoms that have arisen. Have participants compare autogenic relaxation to PMR. Review participants' Daily Self-Monitoring Sheets for adherence. Ask group members:

- "How often do you find you are relaxing?"

- "Where are you practicing relaxation?"

- "What gets in the way for you?"

- "Do you find yourself encountering obstacles to doing relaxation?"

- "What do you say to yourself that keeps you from taking the time to practice relaxation?"

- "What have you done or said to help keep your commitment to relax?"

Diaphragmatic Breathing Review (5 minutes)

Do a quick review of diaphragmatic breathing with the group. Have participants breathe in to the count of 4, hold to the count of 4, exhale to the count of 4, and hold to the count of 4.

Breathe in, 1 . . . , 2 . . . , 3 . . . , 4 . . . Hold, 1 . . . , 2 . . . , 3 . . . , 4 . . .
Breathe out, 1 . . . , 2 . . . , 3 . . . , 4 . . . Hold, 1 . . . , 2 . . . , 3 . . . , 4 . . .
[Repeat several times.]

Remind participants that they can use this kind of breathing to calm down in any situation, without anyone even noticing.

Autogenic Training (30 minutes)

Last session participants learned autogenic formulas for heaviness and warmth. This session introduces sets of instruction for heartbeat, breathing, abdomen, and forehead.

Explain to group members that they will be following the same procedure as last week when autogenic training was introduced. They will lie back on their mats, close their eyes, breathe regularly, and say to themselves the autogenic phrases. They are simply adding new autogenic themes to those that were covered last week.

Autogenic Script for Heartbeat, Breathing, Abdomen, and Forehead

Repeat the autogenic script for heaviness and warmth from Session 5. After completing all the phrases, ending with neck and shoulders, move into the following script.

Now say to yourself three times, "My heartbeat is calm and steady." Feel your heart beating strong and even. With each heartbeat, you become calm and balanced. If you experience any discomfort, change the phrase to: "I am calm and relaxed."

Next move your attention to your breathing and say to yourself three times, "My breathing is slow and steady." Inhale deeply, letting the air fill your lungs and push out your stomach. Exhale slowly, releasing any tension. Feel yourself become calmer with every exhalation.

Now, focus on your abdomen and say to yourself three times, "My abdomen is warm." Feel the warmth spread over your abdomen, creating a relaxing effect. If you have abdominal distress, change the phrase to: "I am calm and relaxed." Continue to breathe deeply as you become more and more relaxed.

Next relax your forehead and facial muscles, saying to yourself three times, "My forehead is cool and calm." Notice the sensations of relaxation. With each breath, feel yourself become calm and relaxed.

Take this feeling of calm and relaxation with you into your day. As you continue to practice this exercise, you will be able to relax more quickly, more deeply.

Now rest for a few minutes as you gradually become more alert. Say to yourself three times, "I am relaxed and alert." Inhale deeply and exhale, letting go of any remaining tension. When you are ready, slowly open your eyes.

Discussion of Autogenic Exercise

- "Was this exercise more difficult for you than last week's exercise with the legs and arms?"

- "Was it easier to feel warmth or to feel heaviness this week?"

- "Was feeling warmth or heaviness easier than feeling muscle tension in PMR?"

Homework (5 minutes)

Have group members practice any of the types of relaxation taught so far in the program (i.e., PMR, breathing, imagery, autogenic training). The only guideline is that participants practice twice a day and record stress levels before and after on the Daily Self-Monitoring Sheet.

STRESS MANAGEMENT: *Productive Coping*

Outline

- Review homework (10 minutes)

- Discuss lifestyle integration (10 minutes)

- Define coping (15 minutes)

- Introduce types of productive coping (10 minutes)

- Introduce types of nonproductive coping (10 minutes)

- Discuss coping strategies (15 minutes)

- Assign homework (5 minutes)

- Hand out Session Evaluation Questionnaire (optional) (5 minutes)

Homework Review (10 minutes)

Check for difficulties with completing Stress Responses and Types of Negative Thoughts Monitoring Sheets or Rational Thought Replacement Sheets. Ask group members to describe:

- A stressful situation they experienced in the past week

- The automatic thoughts generated by that situation

- Different types of cognitive distortions they had in relation to that situation

- How they were able to refute the irrational thoughts/cognitive distortions

Discussion of Lifestyle Integration (10 minutes)

The following questions can be used to help group members integrate appraisals, rational thought replacement, and relaxation techniques into their daily lives. These questions also appear with space provided for answers in the workbook section entitled "Skills Self Check."

- "How do you find you are using stress management and relaxation techniques?"

- "Does breathing and relaxation give you time to come up with more rational appraisals?"

- "When are these techniques not working?"

- "When could you be using these techniques that you're not?"

Definition of Coping (15 minutes)

The term "coping" is often used in relation to dealing with stressful situations, but it may have different meanings for different people. For example, some people use the word "coping" to convey a negative experience (e.g., "I just coped with it"). Statements like this one imply that the person could not do anything about the situation but just put up with or "coped" with it. Others have a more optimistic definition of coping (e.g. "The situation is bad, but fortunately I am able to cope with it"). This kind of statement conveys a sense of mastery over a difficult situation.

This program focuses on the definition of coping that refers to an individual's efforts to manage demands that are appraised as exceeding her resources (Lazarus & Folkman, 1984). An individual may cope with such demands by either changing the way she thinks about the situation (cognitive appraisal) or by altering her behaviors in the situation.

Discuss the definition of coping with the group. Ask group members how they define coping. Have group members talk about their coping resources and the effectiveness of these resources.

Types of Productive Coping (10 minutes)

Productive coping involves strategies that are adaptive, efficient, and likely to yield optimal outcomes. Introduce the two types of productive coping to the group.

Problem-Focused Coping

Problem-focused coping involves changing a problem that is causing distress.

Examples of problem-focused coping include:

- Cognitive problem solving
- Decision making

- Conflict resolution

- Seeking information

- Seeking advice

- Goal setting

Problem-focused coping is particularly useful when a stressor is *controllable*, meaning that taking concrete steps to change the stressor can either reduce or eliminate its intensity (Folkman et al., 1991). For example, one's perception that life is now over because one is infected with HIV can be changed for the better by seeking information about medical treatments available.

Emotion-Focused Coping

Emotion-focused coping involves regulating the emotional response produced by a stressful situation. Examples of emotion-focused coping include:

- Cognitive restructuring (e.g., rational thought replacement)

- Emotional expression (e.g., sharing frustration or fears)

- Behavioral changes (e.g., engaging in pleasant activities)

- Physical stress reduction (e.g., exercising, relaxation, deep breathing)

Emotion-focused coping is most useful when a stressor is *uncontrollable*, meaning that it is beyond our capacity to change or alter (Folkman et al., 1991). When a stressor is uncontrollable (e.g., the fact that one is HIV-infected), people feel particularly upset because they feel that nothing they do will make them feel better about the situation. While it is true that nothing they do will change the actual stressor, there are techniques that they can use to change how they feel about the stressor.

Combining Problem-Focused and Emotion-Focused Coping

Problem-focused and emotion-focused coping are not mutually exclusive; instead, the appropriate use of one can facilitate the use of the other. For example, practicing relaxation (an emotion-focused technique) before a doctor's visit can decrease anxiety. This can help the patient focus better on information presented by the doctor and make a calm, informed treatment choice (a problem-focused technique).

Emphasize to group members that using coping strategies can contribute to their emotional and physical well-being during periods of high stress. Most importantly, the coping response is the part of the stress response that is easiest to observe and ultimately change.

Stress Awareness, Cognitive Appraisals, and Coping Responses

Next, show where coping fits into the model of awareness and appraisal. Refer participants to figure 7.1 in the workbook, or you may want to put the model on a flip chart.

As previously stated, an important element of the appraisal process involves determining which aspects of the immediate stressor are controllable and which are uncontrollable. After the situation has been appraised, an appropriate coping strategy can be selected. Individual differences in

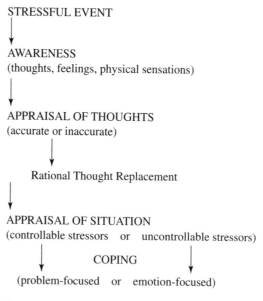

STRESSFUL EVENT

AWARENESS
(thoughts, feelings, physical sensations)

APPRAISAL OF THOUGHTS
(accurate or inaccurate)

Rational Thought Replacement

APPRAISAL OF SITUATION
(controllable stressors   or   uncontrollable stressors)

COPING

(problem-focused   or   emotion-focused)

Figure 8.1

Model of awareness, appraisal, and coping

coping actions and resources play a substantial role in determining how much stress affects a person.

The key to adaptive coping is choosing a strategy that matches the controllability appraisal of the stressor. Changeable aspects of a stressor are best dealt with by problem-focused behaviors, while unchangeable aspects of a stressor may be best dealt with by emotion-focused coping strategies (Folkman et al., 1991). A poor fit between the appraisal of the stressful situation and the coping behaviors employed may decrease the possibility of managing stress and may even increase distress. For example, by concentrating problem-focused efforts on a situation that is uncontrollable, a person remains invested in changing a frustrating situation, which could lead to further distress and fatigue.

Types of Nonproductive Coping (10 minutes)

Next, help group members become more aware of their old, less effective strategies for dealing with difficulties and when these are most likely to arise. These nonproductive strategies are often indirect actions that exist on both the problem-focused and emotion-focused planes. By becoming more aware of the occurrence of these automatic reactions and habitual behaviors, group members may find the entry point for replacing an old ineffective strategy with a new, more effective one. A few of the less productive coping strategies group members may be using are described in the following sections.

Nonproductive Problem-Focused Strategies

These actions involve indirectly approaching the problem. Typically the burden or difficulty is dealt with by forms of avoidance.

Behavioral Avoidance: This includes the great lengths that people will go to in order to reroute their lives away from a person, place, or activity that makes them uncomfortable.

Cognitive Avoidance: This often takes the form of distraction from or outright denial of the problem at hand; it does little to change the nature of the burden. Although denial of ongoing problems (e.g., a new infection, a change in work responsibilities, trouble in a relationship) may be helpful initially in order to deal with overwhelming stressors, the continued use of this cognitive avoidance strategy has been associated with more depression and greater decreases in CD4 (T-helper cell) counts over the subsequent year (Antoni et al., 1991, 1995) and faster disease progression two years later in HIV-positive people (Ironson et al., 1994).

Nonproductive Emotion-Focused Strategies

Other indirect actions tend to be focused on ameliorating the emotional outcome of environmental burdens. These unhealthy behaviors or thoughts, however, often promote, rather than relieve, emotional difficulties. These strategies include:

Consummatory Activities: An increase in activities such as smoking, eating, and alcohol and recreational drug use/abuse may serve, at the physical level, to distract or numb oneself from feelings of anxiety. However, these activities do nothing to alleviate the cause of the anxiety.

Feeling Helpless or Hopeless: When a stressor overwhelms one's energies or resources, one might feel helpless against it or feel hopeless about the future. These kinds of thoughts convey an attitude of "giving up" and may foster depressed mood, pessimism toward the future, and a decreased likelihood of engaging in positive health behaviors.

Engaging in Risky Behaviors: Engaging in risky behaviors (e.g., unprotected sex) is one response to feeling depressed or angry. A person may do this to gain a temporary escape from stressful circumstances and thereby avoid dealing with the source of the stress.

Stuffing Feelings Inside: Not expressing emotions or keeping them "bottled up" may be easier than dealing with them at first but may actually increase depressed feelings in the long run.

Interrelation of Nonproductive Strategies

Nonproductive strategies are interrelated and often perpetuate each other. The use of indirect problem-focused strategies often gives rise to the use of indirect emotion-focused strategies and vice versa. The following example can be used to illustrate this concept to the group:

> *Joe is having a difficult time approaching his supervisor about some recent anxiety-arousing events in which he was discriminated against because of his ethnicity. Anticipating that he will never gain support from his supervisor, he avoids him, feels more anxious, and tries to distract himself from the now recurring problem. As the discriminatory experiences increase in frequency, Joe finds himself eating more junk food and having a few drinks at lunch to "calm down." In this example, Joe's distorted negative thinking encourages avoidance, but since this doesn't solve the problem, he then also engages in consummatory activities to try to reduce his anxious feelings.*

Explain to the group that these nonproductive strategies may make Joe less likely to confront the problem because they:

- Provide temporary relief from the irksome nature of the problem

- Actually reinforce him (with the comfort of food) for escaping from the problem

- Deflate his sense of self-efficacy and self-confidence, thereby making him more likely to avoid, disengage, and distract himself in the future

- Perpetuate feelings of helplessness, increasing the likelihood that Joe may become depressed

Beyond the fact that these indirect strategies may be ineffective for dealing with present difficulties, burdens, and challenges, such indirect strategies may actually increase depressed feelings. Mood states such as depression are associated with poorer functioning of bodily systems such as the immune system (Antoni, 2003).

Table 8.1 Coping Strategies

	Productive	Nonproductive
Problem-Focused	Problem Solving Decision Making Conflict Resolution Seeking Information Goal Setting Seeking Advice	Behavioral Avoidance Cognitive Avoidance/Denial
Emotion-Focused	Cognitive Restructuring Emotional Expression Relaxation Engaging in Pleasant Activities	Consummatory Activities Feeling Helpless or Hopeless Engaging in Risky Behaviors Stuffing Feelings Inside

Discussion of Coping Strategies (15 minutes)

Table 8.1 illustrates the various types of coping that are often used to deal with stressful situations. Direct participants to table 7.1 in the workbook.

Have participants refer to the table and discuss their coping strategies to a situation related to HIV that occurred in the recent past. To facilitate discussion, the following questions may be used:

■ "What are your most common coping strategies?"

■ "Are these productive or nonproductive?"

■ "When do you use more direct (productive) strategies? When do you use more indirect (nonproductive) actions?"

■ "Do you tend to use emotion- or problem-focused strategies?"

Encourage group members to pay attention to their coping strategies in the coming week. In the next session, they will learn the steps involved in executing a desired coping response.

Homework (5 minutes)

✎ Have group members continue to monitor their stress levels at specified times each day and record on the Daily Self-Monitoring Sheet.

✎ Have group members complete the Skills Self-Check in the workbook.

✎ Have group members complete the My Coping Style worksheet in the workbook.

✎ Have group members complete the Coping Response Monitoring Sheet for stressful situations they encounter during the week.

Session Evaluation (optional) (5 minutes)

See example of Session Evaluation Questionnaire at the end of chapter 3.

Chapter 9

Session 7: Autogenic Training with Imagery and Self-Suggestions / Executing Effective Coping Responses

(Corresponds to chapter 8 of the workbook)

Materials Needed

- Autogenic scripts from Sessions 5 and 6

- Relaxation mats

- Flip chart or blackboard

- Copy of the participant workbook

- Copies of audio recording of script for Autogenics with Imagery and Self-Suggestions (optional)

- Copies of audio recording of script for Sunlight Meditation with Autogenics (optional)

- Copies of Matching Coping Behaviors and Appraisals Monitoring Sheet (optional)

- Copies of Daily Self-Monitoring Sheet (optional)

- Copies of Session Evaluation Questionnaire (optional)

Outline

- Discuss home relaxation practice (5 minutes)

- Present rationale for autogenics with imagery and self-suggestions (10 minutes)

- Conduct autogenics with imagery and self-suggestions (25 minutes)

- Conduct sunlight meditation with autogenics (10 minutes)

- Assign homework (5 minutes)

Discussion of Home Relaxation Practice (5 minutes)

Determine and address any difficulties participants have had with practice during the week, or with any symptoms which have arisen. Review participants' Daily Self-Monitoring Sheets for adherence. Ask group members:

- "How often do you find you are relaxing?"

- "Where are you practicing relaxation?"

- "What gets in the way for you?"

- "Do you find yourself encountering obstacles to doing relaxation?"

- "What do you say to yourself that keeps you from taking the time to practice relaxation?"

- "What have you done or said to help keep your commitment to relax?"

Rationale of Autogenic Training with Imagery and Self-Suggestions (10 minutes)

Autogenic training continues in this session with the added components of visual imagery and positive self-suggestions. Adding visual imagery to the physical sensations accompanying autogenic exercises can enhance the relaxation experience by creating a sense of going on an inner journey. Since participants' attention is turned inward, distractions and other external stimuli may be less noticeable. Toward the end of a period of relaxation induction, a person is in a highly suggestible state. Positive self-suggestions made at this time can enhance the efficacy of one's efforts to achieve goals, or change things that one is having difficulty with. Use the following example to illustrate positive self-suggestions to the group:

> *For example, if you want to stop smoking, you could introduce a repeated suggestion such as, "I can do without smoking," or "I enjoy breathing pure air."*

Note that such deliberate suggestions should be brief and to the point, as well as believable. These additional positive self-suggestions may be interspersed with the other autogenic formulas or included at the end of the exercise. General suggestions for centering and increasing the depth of relaxation can also be used, such as the following:

■ *I feel a deep sense of calm*

■ *My whole body feels quite heavy, comfortable, and relaxed*

■ *My mind is quiet; I feel serene and still*

■ *My thoughts are turned inward and I am at ease*

■ *Deep within my mind, I experience myself as calm and peaceful*

Have participants spend a few moments thinking of centering or positive self-suggestions.

Practice of Autogenics with Visual Imagery and Positive Self-Suggestions (25 minutes)

Repeat autogenic scripts from Session 5 and Session 6 and then move directly into the following imagery script (adapted from Mason, 1985). This basic script can be expanded on with additional imagery as time allows. Tell group members, as with any imagery exercise, to feel free if necessary to alter the imagery suggestions to ones that they may find to be more useful or comfortable to work with.

Breathe deeply, releasing tension with every exhalation. Let your thoughts float up and out of your mind. Do not hold onto your thoughts; just let them pass on by. As your mind becomes clear, you become calm and relaxed.

Imagine yourself moving further and further down into relaxation. As you reach the depth of your relaxation, you find yourself surrounded by a calm, peaceful scene. Step into this scene and follow a path to a special place of your own choosing. This may be a place that you have been, or that you would like to go, or that only exists in your imagination.

Pick a comfortable spot and lie down, letting your body sink into the ground. Feel a sense of calm and relaxation. The sun gently shines down on you and warms your hands, your feet, your arms and legs. As the warmth spreads over your body, you feel the tension melting away. You drift deeper into a state of calm and relaxation. Your arms and legs become heavier and heavier, and you sink further into the ground. Enjoy the stillness of your special place.

As you lie comfortable and relaxed, repeat your special phrase to yourself three times. Or say to yourself, "My mind is peaceful. I feel calm and still. My thoughts are turned inward and I am at ease."

Now picture yourself breathing in a gentle healing light of color, whatever color is right for you. This color softly surrounds and heals any part that needs to be healed. Gather the healing energy of your body and bring it to this spot. Imagine this energy restoring your body to health. Stay with this feeling for a few minutes.

Take this feeling of calm and relaxation with you into your day. As you continue to practice this exercise, you will be able to relax more quickly, more deeply.

Now rest for a few minutes as you gradually become more alert. Say to yourself three times, "I am relaxed and alert." Inhale deeply and exhale, letting go of any remaining tension. When you are ready, slowly open your eyes.

Discussion

- "How difficult did you find this exercise compared to the basic autogenic exercise without imagery?"

- "Did you find that the imagery deepened your relaxation?"

- "How did it compare with the imagery we have done earlier?"

- "How well were you able to follow the imagery?"

- "Did you find you needed to change any of the imagery suggestions to make them more powerful for you?"

- "Did your practice since last week make a difference in feeling warmth or heaviness?"

- "How deep a state of relaxation did you feel compared to progressive muscle relaxation? How do you find this compares to PMR for you?"

Tell the group that some people may find visualization quite difficult, but it is a skill that improves with practice. Some people find that using visualization enhances their ability to feel physical sensations such as warmth and heaviness. If this is the case, it would be a good idea to accompany autogenic or progressive muscle relaxation with appropriate visual imagery.

Sunlight Meditation with Autogenics (10 minutes)

Imagine yourself in a scenic outdoor setting. You are safe and relaxed. A warm gentle breeze blows over your body. Overhead, the sky is a beautiful blue with a few white clouds. The light of the sun gently shines down on you. You feel its warmth beginning to relax and soothe every part of your body.

Now imagine that you are moving the sunlight onto your right arm. Concentrate on the warmth as it penetrates your hand, and then moves up your forearm and upper arm all the way to your shoulder. The sunlight warms and soothes your entire right arm. You feel your arm becoming completely relaxed, from the tips of your fingers to your shoulder. Now move the sunlight to your left arm and repeat the sensations of warmth and relaxation.

Next, move the sunlight over to your right leg. Feel the warmth move from the tips of your toes into your foot, up your calf, your knee, your thigh, and all the way up your leg to the hip bone. The sunlight seeps into and soothes every muscle, tendon, and nerve in your right leg. You feel your leg become completely relaxed. Now, move the sunlight to your left leg and repeat the sensations of warmth and relaxation.

Now move the sunlight over your abdomen. Feel it warm and soothe every organ in the lower part of your body. The tensions of the day drain away as you become more and more relaxed. Feel the sense of complete relaxation in your abdomen.

Next, move the sunlight over your chest area. Let the sunlight soothe and comfort as it streams into your chest. Feel your chest relax and your breathing become easy. You are comfortable, relaxed, and at peace. Now take a moment to feel the sensations of warmth and relaxation across your chest, abdomen, arms, and legs. Focus on these sensations for a few minutes.

Every time you practice this exercise you will get better at it, being able to relax more deeply and more completely. You can use this exercise to help you feel calm and relaxed and release tension in your daily life.

Now, gently bring yourself out of deep relaxation to a more alert state, gradually letting yourself become more aware of your surroundings, remaining calm and relaxed.

Discussion Questions

■ "How did this relaxation exercise compare with other exercises we have used in the group?"

■ "What aspects of this exercise were difficult or easy to imagine?"

■ "To date, which of the guided imagery exercises have you most enjoyed?"

■ "Would you incorporate this relaxation exercise into your relaxation schedule?"

Homework (5 minutes)

✎ Have group members practice any of the types of relaxation taught so far in the program (i.e., PMR, breathing, imagery, autogenic training). The only guideline is that participants practice twice a day and record stress levels before and after on the Daily Self-Monitoring Sheet.

STRESS MANAGEMENT: *Executing Effective Coping Responses*

Outline

- ▦ Review homework (10 minutes)

- ▦ Introduce steps to effective coping (30 minutes)

- ▦ Practice effective coping (15 minutes)

- ▦ Introduce softening technique for overwhelming stressors (10 minutes)

- ▦ Conduct softening exercise (5 minutes)

- ▦ Assign homework (5 minutes)

- ▦ Hand out Session Evaluation Questionnaire (5 minutes)

Homework Review (10 minutes)

Give each member the opportunity to describe a stressful event and coping response from the homework (Coping Response Monitoring Sheet). Classify the types of coping used as being problem- or emotion-focused, and productive or nonproductive. Questions to ask include:

- ▦ "What are your most common coping strategies?"

- ▦ "Are your choices more problem-focused or emotion-focused?"

- ▦ "When do you use productive strategies? Nonproductive strategies?"

To begin, review the various types of coping behaviors presented in the last session. Some of these behaviors are more productive over the long run because they allow us to deal actively with the controllable and uncontrollable aspects of stressors that we face. Remind the group that within productive coping strategies, problem-focused coping is generally most useful for dealing with controllable stressors, and emotion-focused coping is most helpful for handling stressors that seem uncontrollable and unmanageable.

In contrast to the productive coping strategies are the nonproductive strategies that also help us to cope with stress, but do so in a less effective manner over the long run. Nonproductive strategies may appear to do a good job of managing our stress in the short term but do little to solve our problems over the long run or help us to deal effectively with troublesome emotions. Like productive strategies, nonproductive strategies deal with controllable and uncontrollable aspects of stress and also can be divided into problem-focused and emotion-focused categories. Review the table on types of coping in Session 6.

Now that group members are familiar with the various types of coping strategies that might be employed to help deal with stress, with your help they can begin discussing ways of using their new skills in cognitive restructuring to more clearly define stressors, decide what aspects of them are controllable and uncontrollable, and select more effective and productive coping strategies to deal with these stressors.

The following steps serve as a useful guide for initiating a productive plan of coping (adapted from Folkman et al., 1991):

Step 1. Break down the stressor into specific situations. A general state of affairs (e.g., a demanding job) is often complex and difficult to cope with, whereas specific stressful situations (e.g., a new large report due) are often less overwhelming and easier to cope with.

Step 2. Identify specific demands of the situation (e.g., what is being required of you, what is being done to you?).

Step 3. Identify controllable and uncontrollable aspects of the situation (i.e., what can be changed? what can't be changed?).

Step 4. Establish goals for coping based on the appropriate fit between coping strategies and appraisal of the situation (i.e., problem-focused strategies for controllable stressors; emotion-focused strategies for uncontrollable stressors).

Practicing Effective Coping (15 minutes)

Breaking Down Qualities of Stressors Exercise

The following exercise provides practice in Steps 1, 2, and 3 of the coping guidelines. To begin, have group members generate examples of a general stressful situation in their lives (e.g., being infected with HIV). Have them identify specific stressful demands of the general situation, as well as identify the controllable and uncontrollable aspects of the problem. For example:

1. Choose a general stressor: Being infected with HIV

2. Identify specific stressful demands:

    - Having frequent doctor appointments

    - Informing your family of your sero-status

    - Adhering to complex medical regimens

    - Negotiating safer sex behaviors with partners

    - Developing a new physical symptom

3. Separate uncontrollable and controllable aspects:

    Controllable:

    - Informing your family of your sero-status

    - Adhering to complex medical regimens

    - Negotiating safer sex behaviors with partners

    Uncontrollable:

    - Having frequent doctor appointments

    - Developing a new physical symptom

Matching Coping Strategies to Stressors

After practicing Steps 1, 2, and 3, Step 4 is to choose an appropriate coping strategy. It is important to match the strategy to a specific aspect of the stressful situation. Remind the group that problem-focused coping is best used when attempting to deal with controllable stressors, and emotion-focused coping is better used when stressors are perceived as being uncontrollable.

Steps to Problem-Focused Coping (for dealing with controllable stressors)

1. Brainstorm options for changing the situation.

2. Consider the possible outcomes of each option.

3. Order the options according to their level of importance.

Examples of Emotion-Focused Coping (for dealing with uncontrollable stressors)

- Do relaxation exercises

- Pursue pleasant activities

- Accept negative emotions instead of avoiding them

Establishing a Coping Plan

The following exercise allows group members to talk about situations that are specifically stressful to them. Participants discuss productive and nonproductive coping strategies associated with a range of stressful situations and brainstorm effective coping plans for those situations. This exercise helps participants to practice all four steps of effective coping.

Part A: Personal Situations

Have participants discuss personal situations that they find to be stressful and explain the coping strategies that they typically use. Allow group members to evaluate their overall coping plan with respect to problem-

and emotion-focused coping. The group can brainstorm new ideas for coping with the stressors discussed.

Part B: HIV-Related Situations

The following stressors are often encountered by HIV-infected individuals. Have group members discuss these general stressors in order to arrive at a productive coping plan to manage these stressors more effectively in the future should they arise.

- Difficulty managing their medication regimen

- Learning of a drop in T-cell count

- A friend or lover's decline in health

- Talking to family members about HIV and AIDS

The key is to help group members to identify the controllable and uncontrollable aspects of each. Some stressors (e.g., death of a friend) have only uncontrollable features; the most appropriate coping responses for these are typically emotion-focused. Others (e.g., difficulty managing medications) may have many controllable elements that can be addressed with problem-focused strategies. Others, such as talking to family members about HIV, may involve a mixture of controllable (e.g., what to say and when) and uncontrollable (e.g., how they react) aspects.

Softening Technique for Overwhelming Stressors (10 minutes)

Tell the group members that sometimes they may encounter overwhelming or uncontrollable stressors that require an immediate response on their part to avoid remaining overwhelmed. One helpful immediate response is acceptance. Acceptance of even the most stressful circumstances may be facilitated with the use of a technique known as "softening." Much of this technique involves changing one's attitude toward unpleasant stimuli, thoughts, or feelings.

Use the example of responding to pain to illustrate this technique to the group. One's attitude towards painful feelings and physical pain is important in determining how much stress one feels. The natural tendency is to brace against pain—to tighten against physical pain and try to block out or avoid emotional pain. The more one attempts to resist pain, however, the more it hurts, setting up a negative feedback cycle.

Explain to the group that tightening tends to increase the sense of physical pain. It also tends to interfere with the ability to deal with emotional pain. One may not like the fact that one is feeling something painful, but opening up to what is there, without judgment, can often bring release and relief from it. By acknowledging one's feelings and experiences, one eliminates the stress of bracing against or running away from them, and allows oneself to use as much energy as possible for coping with life situations directly. By allowing "what is" to be there, one can take in as much information as possible, deal with the reality of the situation, and maximize one's options.

Take the group through the following method on how to soften against pain. This technique can be applied to distressing thoughts, negative emotions, and pain or other physical sensations.

Practicing Softening Against Pain

To "soften" against your physical pain, take a deep breath and relax the muscles around the painful area. As you continue breathing, consciously allow the physical pain to filter into the body, noticing and watching the sensations as they occur. Often this brings a deep sense of release from letting go of tension, and a new awareness that the pain is not as bad as you had anticipated.

To soften around emotional pain, first become aware of the uncomfortable or distressing situation that you may have been avoiding. Do what you can to just let the feelings associated with that situation flow into your body and experience them in a nonjudgmental way. Acknowledge the pain, and adopt an attitude of compassion towards the feelings associated with the pain. This will often bring a sense of release and self-acceptance.

Softening Exercise (5 minutes)

In this exercise, group members practice the technique of softening by simply imagining some person or situation that they are having difficulty with and then allowing themselves to experience any painful feelings that arise rather than brace against them.

Think about someone you have had trouble with. Or think of something you're not looking forward to. Feel the feeling associated with that situation in your body. Just allow that feeling to be, gently, without judging it, and without pulling away from it. You might let yourself put your hand over the place that hurts in a way that almost soothes it, and say quietly to yourself, "This is what I feel right now and it is real."

You will find that the feeling may loosen or release somewhat. Let yourself embrace that feeling as you would a hurt child. Acknowledge whatever attitudes, feelings, or thoughts arise into awareness as you continue to pay attention to the sensation, moment to moment. Stay with this feeling for a few more moments. Then gently bring your awareness back to the room, keeping with you the awareness toward yourself.

Discussion Questions

- "What situation did you imagine in your mind?"

- "What feelings did you notice? Where were they located in your body?"

- "Were you able to sit with those feelings, or did you notice yourself wanting to quickly get rid of them?"

- "Do you often find that you are trying to avoid painful emotions? How do you do this?"

- "What might help you to sit quietly with your painful emotions? Is there a special place that you could go to? Is there certain music that might help facilitate this process?"

- "How often might you want to practice this exercise?"

Homework (5 minutes)

✎ Have group members continue to monitor their stress levels at specified times each day and record on the Daily Self-Monitoring Sheet.

✎ Have group members complete the Breaking Down General Stressors Exercise in the workbook.

✎ Have group members complete the Coping Plan Exercise in the workbook.

✎ Have group members complete the Matching Coping Behaviors and Appraisals Monitoring Sheet for at least three separate stressful situations in the coming week.

Session Evaluation (optional) (5 minutes)

See example of Session Evaluation Questionnaire at the end of chapter 3.

Chapter 10 | *Session 8: Mantra Meditation / Anger Management*

(Corresponds to chapter 9 of the workbook)

Materials Needed

- Autogenic training script from Session 7

- Relaxation mats

- Flip chart or blackboard

- Copy of the participant workbook

- Copies of audio recording of Mantra Meditation script (optional)

- Copies of Anger Awareness Monitoring Sheet (optional)

- Copies of Daily Self-Monitoring Sheet (optional)

- Copies of Session Evaluation Questionnaire (optional)

RELAXATION TRAINING: *Mantra Meditation*

Outline

- Discuss home relaxation practice (5 minutes)

- Review autogenic training with visual imagery (10 minutes)

- Introduce meditation (10 minutes)

- Present postures for meditation (10 minutes)

- Conduct mantra meditation (10 minutes)

■ Discuss benefits of regular meditation practice (10 minutes)

■ Assign homework (5 minutes)

Discussion of Home Relaxation Practice (5 minutes)

Determine and address any difficulties participants have had with practice during the week, or with any symptoms which have arisen. Review participants' Daily Self-Monitoring Sheets for adherence. Ask group members:

■ "How often do you find you are relaxing?"

■ "Where are you practicing relaxation?"

■ "What gets in the way for you?"

■ "Do you find yourself encountering obstacles to doing relaxation?"

■ "What do you say to yourself that keeps you from taking the time to practice relaxation?"

■ "What have you done or said to help keep your commitment to relax?"

Review of Autogenic Training with Imagery and Self-Suggestions (10 minutes)

Review instructions for autogenic training with imagery and self-suggestions. Conduct the imagery exercise again using the script from Session 7. Repeating the exercise helps to reinforce its importance to group members.

Introduction to Meditation (10 minutes)

Definition of Meditation

Define meditation for the group. The following dialogue may be helpful to begin:

Meditation involves focusing attention and awareness. Meditation allows you to have a quiet time to turn your attention within, to steady and center the mind, and to bring a greater sense of quiet awareness to everything that you do. When you center yourself in this way, you can bring a sense of balance to all your activities.

Emphasize that the object of the meditation is less important than the meditative attitude, which is one of uncritical passive awareness. In some forms of meditation, the focus is on a visual image such as a candle flame, or a blank spot on the wall. Other forms of meditation focus on the rising and falling of the breath. Still other forms of meditation use contemplation of visual images or concepts, such as the infinity of the ocean. In a form of meditation known as mindfulness meditation, the meditator is open to awareness of the moment, including all passing thoughts, feelings, sensations, and perceptions, whether sitting quietly or engaged in daily actions.

The form of meditation practiced in this session is called *mantra meditation*, which is the most common form of meditation throughout the world. It involves the repetition, either aloud or silent, of a syllable, a word, or a group of words like "one" or "peace" or "shalom" or "om." Explain to the group that the idea is to develop a focal point that is sounded internally or verbally.

Physiological Effects of Meditation

In the late 1960s and early 1970s, Dr. Herbert Benson and his colleagues at Harvard Medical School studied volunteer practitioners of Transcendental Meditation (Benson, 1976). Benson and others demonstrated that during meditation:

- Heart rate and breathing slow down

- Blood pressure decreases in patients with elevated blood pressure

- Oxygen consumption decreases by 20%

- Levels of blood lactate (which rise during stress and fatigue) drop

- Skin conductance decreases (stress induces sweat, which is a good conductor of electrical charges)

- Alpha brain waves, another sign of relaxation, are increased

Medical Applications of Meditation

Meditation has been used for many medical conditions, including hypertension, muscle tension, pain syndromes, headaches, insomnia, infertility, heart disease, autoimmune conditions (e.g., arthritis and diabetes), skin conditions, asthma, and symptoms related to cancer and HIV. Meditation has also shown to be beneficial in treating emotional conditions such as depression, anxiety, and other disorders.

Although there are many different types of meditation, according to Benson the following conditions seem to be fundamental for physiological change:

- A place to meditate where one will not be disturbed

- An object (word, sound, sensation, image) to serve as a focus of attention

- A passive receptive attitude

- Practicing approximately 20 minutes once or twice daily

The Meditative Attitude

In starting to meditate, most people notice that a host of thoughts will arise, seemingly out of nowhere. These thoughts can easily distract the meditator from his focus. Such a stream of thoughts demonstrates how difficult it is for the mind to stay centered. It may take some time for the meditator to notice that the mind has drifted to other topics. When this happens, the meditator should gently bring the mind back to the object of meditation. This may happen again and again in the course of a meditation.

Ideally, thoughts should be treated like clouds floating by. The meditator is encouraged to watch her thoughts go by on the screen of consciousness, but not to grasp them and turn them over and start to ruminate about them. Letting thoughts go gradually contributes to stilling and centering the mind. This process of passive, nonjudgmental witnessing of thoughts is essential for meditation.

With the practice of meditation comes the ability to distance oneself from habitual patterns of thoughts and emotions, which allows one to develop a new sense of perspective and mental control. The meditator begins to feel much less buffeted by thoughts and emotions, which can improve her well-being.

Postures for Meditation (Derived from Davis et al., 1988) (10 minutes)

Go over the following postures for meditation with the group.

Basic Positions

Sit in a chair, with your feet flat on the floor, your knees comfortably apart, and your hands resting in your lap. Or sit cross-legged on the floor with a cushion under your buttocks so that both knees touch the floor.

Back

Your back should be straight (but not rigid). Let your spinal column directly support the weight of your head. Do this by pulling your chin in slightly. Allow the small of your back to arch.

Balance

Rock briefly from side to side, then from front to back, in order to find your balance. Your upper torso should rest securely on your hips.

Mouth

Close your mouth and breathe through your nose. Let your tongue rest on the roof of your mouth.

Hands

Your hands can rest comfortably in your lap or on your knees, or they can rest open on your knees with your forefingers and thumbs touching.

Breathing

During meditation, diaphragmatic breathing is the most relaxing. Allow deep diaphragmatic breaths to center you as you begin to meditate. You should notice that your breath begins to rest low in your belly, rather than your upper body.

Mantra Meditation Practice (10 minutes)

Before beginning the meditation practice, have participants select a syllable (e.g., "om"), a word (e.g., "one" or "peace"), or a short phrase (e.g., "I am calm") that they would like to use as a mantra. Tell participants that once they have chosen a mantra, they should stay with it throughout their practice, as it will quickly come to be associated with the meditation experience. Use the following script to conduct the meditation (adapted from Mason, 1985):

Get into your meditative position. Take several deep breaths and allow all of the day's activities and concerns to fall away. Do not hold on to any of them. Just let them pass without allowing them to bother you. Begin to focus on your breath, breathing slowly and naturally. Breathe away any thoughts that may be distracting or disturbing you. As your mind becomes clear, you may start to feel calm and relaxed.

Take a moment to scan your body and become aware of any held tension. Focus and release tension in your feet . . . your legs . . . your abdomen . . . your chest . . . your hands . . . your arms . . . your shoulders . . . your neck . . . and your head. Let go of any tension remaining in any part of your body. Now shift your attention back to your breath, which has established its own regular and even pattern.

Begin to repeat your mantra over and over. Let your mantra find its own rhythm; do not force it. Focus on your mantra with minimal effort. Whenever your mind wanders, gently bring it back to your mantra. If you ob-

serve any sensations in your body, just notice them, and then return to the repetition of your mantra. If you have any distracting thoughts, just notice them, and then bring your attention back to your mantra.

Maintain soft awareness of each repetition of your mantra. Remain in this state as long as you want, repeating your mantra at regular intervals until you are completely calm and relaxed. When you are ready to end your meditation, take a deep breath, exhale fully, and open your eyes. You can say to yourself "I am refreshed and alert."

Discussion Questions

■ "How did you find this experience?"

■ "What sort of distractions occurred for you? Were they sounds from the outside? Bodily sensations? Thoughts?"

■ "Did you have any uncomfortable sensations or feelings?"

■ "Was meditation easier or more difficult than previous relaxation exercises like PMR and autogenics?"

■ "How might you adapt this procedure to better suit your individual preferences?"

Benefits of Regular Practice (10 minutes)

Emphasize to the group that regular practice is important to experience the maximum benefits of meditation. Although one can learn to meditate quickly and rapidly experience an increased sense of centeredness, levels of relaxation deepen with practice. In addition, a more sustained sense of centeredness will develop over time as one meditates. With practice, one becomes more adept at experiencing thoughts, sensations, and events without overreacting to them, whether during meditation practice or during the day. When one first begins to meditate, the regularity of practice is most important, even if it is only for five minutes daily. As one becomes more practiced, 20 to 30 minutes once or twice a day is optimal. Tell group members that if they are able to practice for only five to 10 minutes, that is okay: it is better for them to practice a little bit than to skip the day altogether.

Homework (5 minutes)

✎ Have group members practice mantra meditation on a daily basis (twice a day if possible). They should record stress levels before and after each practice on the Daily Self-Monitoring Sheet.

STRESS MANAGEMENT: *Anger Management*

Outline

- ▦ Review homework (10 minutes)

- ▦ Discuss the concept of anger (10 minutes)

- ▦ Facilitate members' self-evaluation of anger (15 minutes)

- ▦ Discuss anger and awareness (10 minutes)

- ▦ Teach anger management (25 minutes)

- ▦ Assign homework (5 minutes)

- ▦ Hand out Session Evaluation Questionnaire (optional) (5 minutes)

Homework Review (10 minutes)

Check for any difficulties with self-monitoring of coping strategies. Review group members' stressful situations from the past week. Identify and assess the practicality of the coping styles used. Look for instances where passive strategies were used when more active ones could have been substituted.

Ask if participants could recognize the difference between uncontrollable stressors and controllable ones. Review which coping style works best for each type of stressor (i.e., problem-focused coping for controllable stressors; emotion-focused coping for uncontrollable stressors).

Discussion of Anger Responses (10 minutes)

Discuss the concept of anger with the group (portions of this anger management module were adapted from Ironson, Lutgendorf, Starr, & Costello [1989]). One aspect of stress management is learning how to deal with negative situations, including those in which one has been unfairly treated, slighted, or offended by others in some way. A very reasonable emotional response to these kinds of situations is anger. Anger can manifest in healthy ways that motivate the person to take corrective actions. Anger can also occur in less healthy ways ranging from "stuffing one's feelings" on one extreme to "explosive responses" on the other. This module teaches ways to become more aware of anger-inducing situations, how one experiences anger, and optimal ways to express anger and take corrective actions. These techniques are collectively referred to as anger management. Questions to ask the group during your discussion include:

- "How do you define anger?"
- "How do you know when you are angry?"
- "What negative connotations are associated with anger?"
- "What associations do you have with overcontrolled or uncontrolled anger?"

Reiterate that a healthy attitude includes the understanding that anger is a normal human emotion.

Self-Evaluation of Anger (15 minutes)

The following exercise helps participants to better understand anger in both themselves and others, and allows them to increase their awareness of how anger both positively and negatively affects them in their present lives. Have participants fill out the Self-Evaluation Questionnaire in their workbooks.

Discussion of Self-Evaluation Questionnaire

After participants have completed the Self-Evaluation Questionnaire, guide them in discussing what they learned from this exercise. Use the following questions:

Questions for General Exploration

- "What did you learn about anger when you were young?"

- "Has that carried over into your relationships today?"

- "Is the expression of anger difficult for you?"

- "What happened when you were a child and you expressed your anger?"

- "Do you ever feel out of control with your anger?"

- "Do you ever suppress your feelings of anger?"

- "Do you think that expressing anger is good or bad?"

Questions about Personal Triggers for Anger

- "What causes you to be angry?"

- "What are your personal anger triggers?"

Some common responses may be frustration, harassment, disappointments, being hurt, being HIV-infected, deadlines, doctors' lack of understanding, intolerance, people's lack of consideration, people not doing what one wants.

Anger and Awareness (10 minutes)

The following are some issues for participants to consider before they are in an acute event that makes them angry. This discussion will help them to become more aware of anger-inducing situations and their initial responses to these situations. Emphasize that it is important for partici-

pants to become aware before they become upset or less able to be ana-
lytical and objective about the situation.

Awareness of the Physical Symptoms of Anger

Unfortunately, many people do not recognize that they are really angry
until their anger is completely out of control. One of the easiest ways to
become aware that we are angry about something is to become aware of
the physical symptoms that typically arise when we are angry. For example, some of the physical consequences of anger might include:

- Increased blood pressure

- Increased blood flow

- Increased heart rate

- Increased muscle tension

Explain to group members that becoming aware of these physical symptoms as they arise might tip them off to the fact that they are really angry
about something. Increasing early awareness of anger symptoms will
allow them to deal more effectively with their feelings of anger.

It is also useful to think about what happens in our bodies when we do
not express our anger but instead let angry feelings build up until they
are unmanageable. Since we are actually responding internally to the
stressful situation, many of the physical changes noted earlier (e.g., increase in blood pressure) occur. The following questions are designed to
help group members think about what happens to them physically when
they do not express feelings of irritation, annoyance, and anger on a regular basis.

- "What happens when you suppress your anger?"

- "Where does all that energy go?"

- "What might that mean for you physically?"

- "Do you have any physical discomfort that might be associated
  with unresolved anger?"

Awareness of Patterns of Responding

Next help group members recognize their characteristic patterns and vulnerabilities when responding to situations that induce anger. Have them refer to one of the situations that they endorsed on the Self-Evaluation Questionnaire.

- ▓ "Where do you get that pattern from?"

- ▓ "How effective is your typical pattern for dealing with situations?"

- ▓ "Do you tend to be upset or relieved after you respond in this way?"

- ▓ "Are you usually happy with the outcome?"

- ▓ "Do you want to change the pattern or is it okay?"

When confronted with a situation, it is also important to recognize the other person's characteristic patterns and vulnerabilities—that is, when we react to an anger-inducing situation, we are not the only one being affected. Our response itself may trigger angry feelings in those around us. The consequences of our decisions to express our anger may differ based on the nature of the relationship, so part of raising our awareness includes being more aware of the ways our responses affect others and the consequences that can have on the relationship.

Awareness of the Power Dynamics of the Situation

Explain to the group that another step of awareness is recognizing one's position of power in the situation. The amount of power a person holds can vary in different relationships (e.g., in one's relationship with a boss versus with a colleague who is at an equal or subordinate position within the company). The degree to which a person expresses angry feelings must be determined in the context of his relative power in the relationship. With persons in a superordinate position (over one), like the boss, the consequences of a confrontation may not be worth the potential benefits.

Tell group members that they might also ask themselves whether they want to continue a relationship with a particular individual when deciding upon confrontation (e.g., ask, "Is this your best friend or the bank teller?"). In closer, more long-standing relationships, one may be willing to share deeper expressions of feelings than in casual interactions. The hope is that the person will modify her behavior in the future of their continuing relationship. In a casual interaction, the likelihood of ever interacting again with that person is low, so the value of sharing personal feelings is not likely worth the investment.

Awareness of Other External and Internal Factors

There may also be additional factors that are contributing to an aggravating situation. For instance when people are sick, tired, or hungry, they may become quickly irritable in demanding situations. This may lead them to react in a less rational manner, a response that they may later regret. Provide the group with the following questions to help recognize these factors.

Recognition of External Factors

- "Are there extenuating circumstances or reasons why someone might be creating difficulties for you?"

- "Have you failed to resolve an old issue with this person?"

- "Have you heard from others that this person 'has it out' for you?"

- "Have there been a number of demands in the situation that have accumulated?"

- "Has the situation caught you off guard? Do you need a few minutes to collect your thoughts?"

Recognition of Internal Factors

- "Are you hungry?"

- "Have you had enough sleep?"

- "Are you sick? Do you have a cold, headache, etc.?"

- "Which of your 'buttons' are being pushed?"

- "What is setting you off?"

- "What issues make you sensitive to feeling angry?"

Anger Management (25 minutes)

Now that participants are aware of their typical symptoms of anger and automatic reactions, they can begin to devise ways to slow down the automatic anger process and manage anger more effectively.

Slowing Down the Automatic Anger Process

- *Recognize the thoughts you are having about the situation before you react. Do you feel offended by a person? Unfairly treated by a person or organization? Frustrated by a turn of events?*

- *Notice physical symptoms of anger—these are cues that you are being emotionally affected by the situation.* (Review symptoms presented earlier in the session.)

- *Acknowledge your anger (don't invalidate your emotion). Attempting to suppress your anger will not alter the physical effects you are experiencing and may delay you from taking action to end the aggravating event or behavior.*

- *If you are too upset or angry to deal with situation appropriately, take time to cool down or use a buffer (e.g., exercise, talking it over) before dealing with the situation.*

Anger Appraisal

The process of cognitive restructuring learned in previous weeks can be useful in learning to better manage anger. Teach participants to examine thought processes, identify where distorted negative thoughts cause unnecessary anger, and change these negative thoughts to more rational and realistic thoughts. The following questions may be useful in beginning this process of cognitive restructuring:

- "What are things you say to yourself (thoughts) that make you angry?"

- "What is the valid part of your anger?"

- "Do you have any distorted thoughts contributing to or exacerbating your experience of anger?" (e.g., "No one treats me with respect;" "Everyone steps on me.")

- "What are more rational and realistic thoughts that may decrease your anger?"

Tell group members that in addition to better understanding how their own thoughts cause them unnecessary anger and distress, they might also want to think about what the other person (who is contributing to their anger) might be experiencing. Respecting and understanding the other person's position can go a long way toward reducing the level and intensity of conflicts, which ultimately can reduce anger.

When angry at another person, participants may want to ask themselves the following questions:

- "Where is the other person coming from?"

- "Is the other person 'off the wall?'"

- "What might I be doing to make the other person angry?"

- "Is it possible that the other person might be right in her actions and I might be wrong in my interpretation of what is going on?"

The following four steps (ASAP) can help participants gain a better understanding of what is making them angry, what options they have for dealing with the anger, and managing the anger in an effective manner.

Questions to Ask Yourself ASAP

Awareness: "Who or what am I really angry with or about?"

Source: "Why? What is the real source of my anger?"

Alternatives: "What do I want to do? Do I have alternatives for accomplishing the same thing?"

Plan: "What is my plan of action?"

Expressing Anger: What Are Your Options?

In learning the best ways to express anger, there are two main considerations. One concerns choosing a strategy; the other is having alternative options available. Discuss these with the group.

Strategy Tips

- Recognize your needs

- Recognize the needs of the other person

- Assess timing (Do you need to be in a better mood to say something about this? Does the other person need to be in a better mood?)

- Establish the desired outcome (Do you want to salvage the relationship? Do you want to reach a certain goal no matter what it does to the relationship?)

- Determine the power differences in the relationship (Who holds the power in this situation? Are you above or below this person, or are you on an equal footing?)

- Determine the nature of the continuing relationship (Are you close to this person? Will you have a future relationship with this person?)

Alternative Options

When you are in the process of expressing your anger, be aware that there are more possibilities than stuffing your anger or blowing up. Start to learn which other ways of dealing with anger work for you. Begin with the following list. Have you found any of these to be useful alternatives to stuffing anger or blowing up? Some of these alternatives are useful when you need to defer your confrontation to a later time. Do any of these alternatives seem to be less effective than others for you?

- Assertiveness (e.g., "When you do Y, I feel X.")

- Cooling down (i.e., waiting for a better time)

- Defusing (e.g., seeking advice)

- Exercise (e.g., going for a walk)

- Expression (e.g., informing the person that you think you are being treated unfairly)

- Information seeking (i.e., getting more details about the situation or what the person is communicating)

Now that participants understand that a variety of options exist for managing anger, they may complete the exercise in the workbook entitled "Recognizing and Changing Your Typical Anger Pattern." Give group members a few minutes to complete their responses. Then spend some time discussing some of the situations that lead them to feel angry and some of the anger responses that they often experience in these situations. Have other group members brainstorm new ways of coping with these anger-provoking situations while you facilitate the discussion. The goal is to help participants learn that they do not need to stay stuck in the same old patterns of responding to situations that make them angry, but that alternatives exist that allow for more productive and efficient resolutions to situations that evoke anger responses.

Homework (5 minutes)

✎ Have group members continue to monitor their stress levels at specified times each day and record on the Daily Self-Monitoring Sheet.

✎ Have group members review their answers to the Self-Evaluation Questionnaire: Developing Awareness of Anger.

✎ Have group members review the exercise in the workbook entitled "Recognizing and Changing Your Typical Anger Pattern."

✎ Have group members use the Anger Awareness Monitoring Sheet to record the anger responses that they are most aware of in situations during the next week.

Session Evaluation (optional) (5 minutes)

See example of Session Evaluation Questionnaire at the end of chapter 3.

Chapter 11 | *Session 9: Breath Counting Meditation / Assertiveness Training*

(Corresponds to chapter 10 of the workbook)

Materials Needed

- Sunlight meditation script from Session 7

- Relaxation mats

- Flip chart or blackboard

- Copy of the participant workbook

- Copies of audio recording of script for Breath Counting Meditation (optional)

- Copies of Interpersonal Style Monitoring Sheet (optional)

- Copies of Daily Self-Monitoring Sheet (optional)

- Copies of Session Evaluation Questionnaire (optional)

RELAXATION TRAINING: *Breath Counting Meditation*

Outline

- Discussion of home relaxation practice (5 minutes)

- Conduct breath counting meditation (20 minutes)

- Conduct sunlight meditation with autogenics (10 minutes)

■ Discussion of meditation exercises (10 minutes)

■ Assign homework (5 minutes)

Discussion of Home Relaxation Practice (5 minutes)

Determine and address any difficulties participants have had with meditation practice during the week, or with any symptoms that have arisen. Review participants' Daily Self-Monitoring Sheets for adherence. Ask group members:

■ "How often do you find you are relaxing?"

■ "Where are you practicing relaxation?"

■ "What gets in the way for you?"

■ "Do you find yourself encountering obstacles to doing relaxation?"

■ "What do you say to yourself that keeps you from taking the time to practice relaxation?"

■ "What have you done or said to help keep your commitment to relax?"

Breath Counting Meditation (20 minutes)

This meditation technique (adapted from Davis et. al, 1988, and Mason, 1985) uses the breath in order to deepen the relaxation state. Explain to the group that in breath counting meditation, the breath is the object of focus. Instruct participants to concentrate on their breaths and count from one through 10 on successive inhalations and exhalations. Use the following script to conduct the exercise:

Get in a comfortable position. Take several long, deep breaths and begin to clear your mind. Let go of all the worries and concerns of the day. Close your eyes or fix them on a spot on the floor in front of you. You can either keep your eyes focused or let them go out of focus.

Take deep breaths and focus your attention on each part of the breath. First focus on the inhale. Then focus on the point at which you stop inhaling and start exhaling. Next focus on the exhale. Lastly focus on the pause between the exhale and the next inhale. Pay careful attention to the sensations in your body as you pause between breaths.

As your breathing finds a comfortable rhythm, turn your attention from your abdomen to the passage of the air through your nostrils. Be fully aware as the air comes through your nostrils and as it exits out through your nostrils. On your next breath, pause for just a moment after the inhalation. Become aware of the cool flow of air into your nostrils as you inhale. On the exhale, feel the warm flow of air out of your nostrils.

Begin to count your breaths on the exhale. Inhale . . . Exhale 1 . . . Inhale . . . Exhale 2 . . . Continue counting up to 10, and then start over at 1. If any thoughts come to mind, just let them pass through you. Do not judge or engage with them; just allow them to come and go. If you lose your focus of attention, relax your breathing and start over at the count of 1. If you start to lose count for any reason, just go back to the number 1.

If you begin to breathe unnaturally, to hyperventilate, or to hold your breath, just attempt to relax all the muscles in your chest and abdomen. You can always return to the easy rhythm of your own breath, the sound of air entering and leaving your body, the feeling of air at your nostrils. Then go back to your counting.

Repeat the counting sequence (inhale . . . exhale 1 . . .) for 20 minutes, adding imagery related to the physical sensations of breathing, and the feel and temperature of the inhalations and exhalations. Gradually slow the pacing of your instructions so the breathing slows over this period. End the meditation with:

We have come to the end of this meditation. At your own pace, begin to bring your awareness back to the room. As you practice becoming more aware of your breath, more aware of yourself, the benefits of this practice will expand, so that you can bring full attention to whatever you do during the rest of the day.

Sunlight Meditation with Autogenics (10 minutes)

Using the script from Session 7, repeat the sunlight meditation with autogenics. Mention to participants that they can also combine breathing instructions with autogenics to achieve an even deeper sense of relaxation.

Discussion Questions (10 minutes)

Ask participants to think about how they felt after the breathing exercise and then again after the sunlight meditation. Use the following questions in your discussion:

■ "How was this breath counting meditation exercise for you?"

■ "Was the sunlight imagery experience different for you this time?"

■ "What did you find easy and difficult about this experience?"

■ "How does meditation compare with autogenics or guided imagery?"

■ "Which relaxation exercise did you like most?"

Homework (5 minutes)

✎ Have group members practice breath counting meditation on a daily basis (twice a day if possible). They should record stress levels before and after each practice on the Daily Self-Monitoring Sheet.

STRESS MANAGEMENT: *Assertiveness Training*

Outline

■ Review homework (10 minutes)

■ Introduce interpersonal styles (10 minutes)

■ Discuss barriers to assertive behavior (15 minutes)

- Present components of assertive communication (20 minutes)

- Discuss using problem solving with conflicts (25 minutes)

- Review steps to more assertive behavior (5 minutes)

- Assign homework (5 minutes)

- Hand out Session Evaluation Questionnaire (optional) (5 minutes)

Homework Review (10 minutes)

Determine if group members had any problems monitoring anger responses.

Discuss situations that elicited anger from participants in the last week and how they managed their anger. Identify responses that could be replaced with more effective strategies. Go through the steps to anger management as presented in the last session.

Interpersonal Styles (10 minutes)

Last session dealt with interpersonal skills to better communicate negative emotions such as anger. This session focuses on other interpersonal techniques to better communicate one's needs and desires in different situations. These techniques are collectively referred to as assertiveness skills. One of the first steps in learning assertiveness skills is to become more aware of the different interpersonal styles that one can use in communicating.

When people's intentions are not clearly communicated, then stressful interpersonal conflict may occur. Learning how to communicate assertively with others is a very important component of stress management training. This module demonstrates how passive, aggressive, and passive-aggressive interactions either turn people off or deny them the ability to communicate their needs effectively. After illustrating ineffective (passive or aggressive) communication patterns, you will introduce the group to a more effective communication strategy (i.e., assertiveness).

The following diagram explains the four basic interpersonal styles (you may want to put these on a flip chart). For each style, the communication pattern is defined and the pros and cons are given. It is important to recognize that each communication pattern produces both rewards and costs for the individual. Explain to the group that it's our nature to seek to change unhealthy patterns only when the costs begin to outweigh the benefits. It is important to note that these "costs" may involve added stress that can result from unclear communications.

Four Basic Interpersonal Styles

1. *Aggressive:* Standing up for one's rights by denying feelings of other people

   (+) *Advantage:* People usually don't push an aggressive person around.

   (−) *Disadvantage:* People avoid an aggressive person.

2. *Passive:* Indirectly violating one's own rights by failing to express honest feelings and beliefs

   (+) *Advantage:* Passive individuals rarely experience direct rejection.

   (−) *Disadvantage:* Other people end up making choices for the passive individual, making it hard for the individual to achieve personal goals. Passivity also leads to built-up resentment and guilt for not taking care of oneself.

3. *Passive-Aggressive:* Indirectly and passively resistant

   (+) *Advantage:* A passive-aggressive person avoids direct conflict.

   (−) *Disadvantage:* Passive-aggressiveness can often cause more interpersonal conflict than directly approaching a situation or person.

4. *Assertive:* Standing up for rights and expressing individual feelings and beliefs in a direct way that does not violate rights of others

   (+) *Advantage:* One can choose one's own goals, not turn people off, promote self-efficacy and self-esteem, and decrease interpersonal conflict.

(−) *Disadvantage:* People who are less comfortable or familiar with the direct expression of feelings and desires may withdraw from or grow anxious or irritable during an exchange with an assertive person.

Interpersonal Style Role-Play Exercise

As the group leaders, briefly role-play the following examples of interpersonal style. Have group members identify the interpersonal style used in each situation and come up with alternative assertive responses.

Aggressive Role Play

You've purchased merchandise that is defective and you storm into the store on a busy Saturday afternoon and loudly complain to the salesperson and call him a liar.

Passive Role Play

You are waiting in line and you are in a hurry and someone cuts in front of you. You do nothing.

Passive-Aggressive Role Play

Someone asks to borrow some money from you. You are uncomfortable about this request but grudgingly agree to give him the money tomorrow. Tomorrow comes and you conveniently forget to bring the money with you.

Alternative Assertive Responses

Discuss each of the above examples using the following questions:

- "What behaviors helped you identify the interpersonal style?"
- "Can you think of descriptions for these individuals?"

- "How would you feel acting that way?"

- "What are some alternative assertive responses for this situation?"

After the exercise, have participants think of a situation they encountered over the past week where they or someone else communicated in a nonassertive way. The following questions can be used in your discussion:

- "Can you recall the situation, what was said, and how the receiving party reacted?"

- "How would you classify the person's communications? Passive? Passive-aggressive? Aggressive?"

- "What alternative form of communicating could they use? How would an assertive communication sound?"

- "How are the parties likely to feel afterward?"

Barriers to Assertive Behavior (15 minutes)

There tend to be two main reasons why people act nonassertively or aggressively. First, these individuals often misinterpret the meaning of assertive behavior (e.g., people who use passive styles think there is no way to be assertive without appearing pushy). Second, individuals who have difficulty displaying assertive behaviors often have irrational (and inaccurate) thoughts and beliefs. Go over with the group common examples of negative thinking and cognitive distortions that prevent assertive behavior.

Fear of Displeasing Others

When others disapprove of us, it may be unpleasant and uncomfortable. If we incorrectly interpret disapproval to mean that we are completely bad, we are more likely to become depressed and less likely to stand up for our rights.

Fear of Rejection or Retaliation

Often, our reaction to this fear is more immobilizing than the fear itself. When faced with the possibility of rejection or retaliation, we often see ourselves as helpless. We forget that we do not have to passively accept inappropriate treatment. We can protect ourselves or we can do things for ourselves that would make the rejection easier to face.

Mistaken Sense of Responsibility

When we internalize others' hurt feelings, we take on the responsibility of making everyone else happy. When another person is hurt by your being assertive, it is important to discern whether you actually hurt the other person or whether the other person felt hurt because of his misinterpretation of your assertive behavior.

Mistaken View of Your Human Rights

Many people believe that they don't have the right to stand up for their wants, needs, and wishes. It is very difficult to be assertive when you are denying yourself basic rights. Remember, you can accept and act on your own rights without violating the rights of others.

Reluctance to Forfeit Advantages of Being Nonassertive

It may be important to assess what benefits you may gain when acting nonassertively (e.g., if you don't stand up for your rights, others may defend you and you are still safe; by never disagreeing, you can appear to be easy to get along with).

Feeling Vulnerable and Unsafe

Anger and aggression are often manifested in a person who feels threatened and powerless. It is important to be aware of situations in which you may feel vulnerable, making you more likely to lash out. By preparing yourself for these situations you can stay focused on any irrational thoughts that could cause you to communicate in an aggressive manner.

Emphasize to group members that in order to promote assertive instead of aggressive behavior, it is important that they monitor their thoughts for negative self-statements and cognitive distortions.

Discussion Questions

- ▨ "Did you identify with any of the common barriers to assertive behavior?"

- ▨ "What are some of your reasons why you do not behave assertively?"

- ▨ "When do you behave nonassertively? Any recent situations come to mind?"

- ▨ "Are you able to predict the situations where nonassertive responses are more likely to occur in your life?"

- ▨ "Who are the people with whom you act nonassertively? What is it about them or your expectation about them that affects the way you communicate?"

Components of Assertive Communication (20 minutes)

There are several components to assertive communication. Explain that one of the most important components is the choice of words. You can use the following dialogue for explanation:

Taking ownership of a request by using the pronoun "I" at the beginning of a sentence communicates that you are being proactive and clear about what you want to say. The rest of the sentence should similarly convey clearly what it is that you sense or feel and what it is that you want. This might be something you want to see changed, decreased, or increased. Assertive communications also acknowledge your empathy toward the other person—where he might be coming from, what he might be feeling, and what his desires might include. This is typically followed with a statement about what you would like to see happen. By stringing together several such sentences you will be able to communicate assertively in all types of situations.

Some of the components of communicating assertively are summarized as follows.

"I" Language

Messages in the "I" language are good ways to express negative feelings in a nonblaming way. When using these statements you can point out how others' behaviors concretely affect you while owning your own feelings about the situation. Compare the two examples:

Blaming "You" Message: "When you are late from work, you make me feel insecure."

Assertive "I" Message: "When you are late from work, I often doubt myself and feel insecure about the relationship."

"I Want" Statements

Clarify what you really want, which allows the other person to understand how to fulfill your wants. For example, "I want to eat dinner on time tonight."

"I Feel" Statements

Clarify how you feel without blaming or attacking the other person. To facilitate communication, don't use generalizations to describe how you feel; instead, be specific and quantify your feelings (e.g., extremely happy, slightly irritated). For example, "I feel slightly irritated when you don't call to let me know you'll be late."

Empathic Assertion

This type of message contains two statements. The first statement recognizes the other person's situation, feelings, beliefs, and wants. The second statement asserts your wants, feelings, and beliefs. This message communicates sensitivity for the other person without a total disregard for your rights. For example, "I know that you have a lot of work to get finished and that it is difficult for you to gauge when it will be done, but I need you to call if you are going to be late so I can organize my own schedule this evening."

Effective Listening

Explain to participants that listening to others often encourages others to listen to one more attentively. In addition, effective listening reduces the likelihood that one will misinterpret the message. Effective listening does not mean one is passively agreeing with the other person's message; instead, it means respecting the rights of the sender to express his thoughts and feelings. Effective listening usually consists of *paraphrasing* the content of the message and *nonverbal communication* that one is attentive (e.g., making eye contact, leaning forward, saying "uh-huh," etc.).

> *For example, saying, "It sounds like you are really angry with me and want to avoid having a problem like this occur again" might be an effective way of letting the other person know that you understand that he is upset and wants a resolution to a given problem. Being open to others' comments and criticisms is much more effective in terms of fostering good communication than blowing up, refusing to listen, or accusing the other person of something in order to reduce your feelings of guilt or hurt.*

Exercise: Making Assertive Statements and Listening Effectively

Have participants refer to the exercise in the workbook entitled "Making Assertive Statements and Listening Effectively." Have a group member assertively state each situation while the others listen. Then group members should brainstorm answers to the questions provided in the workbook. These questions are designed to provide group members with practice in coming up with more effective communication strategies to resolve common problems such as the examples given.

Using Problem Solving with Conflicts (25 minutes)

Finding Workable Solutions

Sometimes we must deal with situations that are more vague in terms of what the actual messages, desires, and feelings of the two parties are. Tell group members that they can apply what they have learned about making assertive statements to problem-solving conflicts using the following steps:

1. Recognize there is a problem and define it in clear terms. Be specific and avoid generalizations.

2. Identify possible solutions. Both parties should generate a variety of possible solutions.

3. Critique each possible solution. It is important to be assertive, but remember that the best solution will meet both parties' needs.

4. Accept a solution. Both parties should discuss the expected outcomes and possible barriers to implementing the solution.

Problem-Solving Role-Play

Recall the example of difficulty with a partner who does not listen effectively used in Situation 1 of the exercise entitled "Making Assertive Statements and Listening Effectively." Have two group members role-play this situation in front of the group. In the first role-play, have group members demonstrate the old and ineffective pattern of communication, where one partner does not listen and the other partner becomes increasingly frustrated. In the second role-play, have the two group members use more effective, assertive communication styles in order to bring up this communication problem, use the problem-solving steps, and resolve the situation in a manner agreeable to both parties. After the two role-plays are completed, have the other group members add their comments and suggestions.

Barriers to Conflict Resolution

Many things can get in the way of a successful resolution; however, many of these barriers reflect *inaccurate beliefs* about conflict, such as:

- There is always a winner and a loser

- Direct conflict is to be avoided at all cost

- All conflicts must be resolved

- One person is all right and the other is all wrong

This type of self-talk needs to be challenged and replaced with more rational and less extreme statements. Work with group members to brainstorm other, less extreme statements that could replace each of the above statements. Here are some examples:

- Each person can walk away from a conflict having learned something

- Direct conflicts can take a lot of out you but are sometimes productive in taking care of things before they fester and turn into resentments

- Sometimes people just agree to disagree

- Usually neither person is 100% correct in a conflict

Unsolvable Problems

There may be situations in which no workable solution is available or the risk of being assertive is too great. In such cases there are alternatives to directly assertive behavior, such as changing one's environment, developing ways of satisfying oneself, and tending to one's emotional needs. Remind participants that assertive communication is just one of the many coping strategies available to them. In Sessions 6 and 7, they learned about ways to manage and cope with controllable and uncontrollable stressful situations. Using these other coping strategies in addition to assertive communication will increase the likelihood of their having successful outcomes when experiencing interpersonal difficulty.

Steps to More Assertive Behavior (5 minutes)

1. Be able to identify the four interpersonal styles: passive, passive-aggressive, aggressive, and assertive.

2. Identify situations in which you want to be assertive.

3. Plan for change:

   ▪ Look at both your and the other person's rights, wants, and needs

   ▪ Determine the desired outcome

   ▪ Arrange a time and place to discuss the situation calmly

4. Define feelings using "I" messages. Express your request simply, firmly, and concisely.

5. Increase the possibility of getting what you want by being empathetic about the other person's position.

6. Use body language that conveys that you are attentive.

7. Learn to listen:

   ▪ Make sure you are ready to listen

   ▪ Listen to and clarify what the other person said

   ▪ Acknowledge what was said: communicate to the other person that you have heard his position

8. Be aware of barriers to assertive behavior, including counterproductive self-talk such as:

   ▪ "My behavior will hurt someone else's feelings or they'll reject me"

   ▪ "My job should be to make people happy and comfortable"

   ▪ "In any conflict there has to be a winner and a loser"

Homework (5 minutes)

✎ Have group members continue to monitor their stress levels at specified times each day and record on the Daily Self-Monitoring Sheet.

✎ Have group members complete the exercise in the workbook entitled "Practicing Alternative Assertive Responses."

✎ Have group members complete the Self-Check for Barriers to Assertive Behavior.

Have group members review the exercise in the workbook entitled "Making Assertive Statements and Listening Effectively."

Have group members complete the Interpersonal Style Monitoring Sheet for each problematic situation they encounter this week. They should try for a minimum of three situations.

Session Evaluation (optional) (5 minutes)

See example of Session Evaluation Questionnaire at the end of chapter 3.

Chapter 12 | *Session 10: Imagery and Meditation / Social Support and Review of the Program*

(Corresponds to chapter 11 of the workbook)

RELAXATION TRAINING: *Imagery and Meditation*

Materials Needed

- Beach scene imagery script from Session 3

- Breath counting meditation script from Session 9

- Relaxation mats

- Flip chart or blackboard

- Copy of the participant workbook

- List of resources

- Copies of maintenance calendar (optional)

- Copies of Daily Self-Monitoring Sheet (optional)

- Copies of Session and Program Evaluation Questionnaires (optional)

Outline

- Discuss home relaxation practice (5 minutes)

- Review relaxation exercises (5 minutes)

- Conduct beach scene imagery exercise (20 minutes)

- Conduct meditation exercise (15 minutes)

- Discussion of relaxation exercises (10 minutes)

Discussion of Home Relaxation Practice (5 minutes)

Determine and address any difficulties participants have had with meditation practice during the week, or with any symptoms that have arisen. Review participants' Daily Self-Monitoring Sheets for adherence. Ask group members:

- "How often do you find you are relaxing?"

- "Where are you practicing relaxation?"

- "What gets in the way for you?"

- "Do you find yourself encountering obstacles to doing relaxation?"

- "What do you say to yourself that keeps you from taking the time to practice relaxation?"

- "What have you done or said to help keep your commitment to relax?"

Introduction and Review (5 minutes)

Tell the group that this week they will work with two relaxation exercises that they have previously practiced. The first exercise is the Beach Scene Imagery (ocean or lake) used during Session 3. The second exercise is the breathing meditation completed in Session 9. During this week's session, the group will move directly from the Beach Scene Imagery into the meditation exercise with no break in between. Aside from this minor change, follow the same instructions used during previous weeks when repeating these exercises. Explain to the group that by doing an imagery exercise together with breathing meditation, the effects of relaxation can be deepened and prolonged.

Beach Scene Imagery (20 minutes)

Remember that there are two imagery options for the beach scene, one involving an ocean and the other a lakefront. Choose whichever scene the group members can most easily identify with. Use the script from Session 3.

When the exercise has been completed, have group members keep their eyes closed and remain comfortably relaxed. Move directly into the breathing meditation exercise.

Breathing Meditation (15 minutes)

Immediately follow the beach scene imagery exercise with breathing meditation. Use the Breathing Meditation script from Session 9.

Discussion of Relaxation Exercises (10 minutes)

Have participants discuss their experiences with the beach scene imagery and breathing meditation. Have them describe their thoughts, emotions, and physical sensations during these exercises. Ask them which exercise they enjoyed more. Determine which aspects of these exercises were particularly easy or difficult for them to utilize. Ask participants whether they wish to modify these procedures for home use, and discuss how such modifications would be made.

Remind group members that instructions for all the relaxation exercises are included in their workbook. This allows them to read through the instructions, and then simply close their eyes and guide themselves through the experience. It might take several practice attempts until they feel comfortable guiding themselves through the exercise with no help from the group leader. Emphasize that with continued practice, they should have no difficulty at all doing the exercises on their own. If they do experience difficulties using this approach, they can be encouraged to record themselves reciting the relaxation scripts and then playing this back whenever they wish to do an exercise. Suggest to them that using headphones when listening to the recording during the exercise will work best as it will minimize ambient sounds.

At this point state that this is the last session and now is the time for participants to start planning for a regular routine of relaxation practice that they can engage in after the program has ended. Make sure participants have a continued plan for relaxation practice at home. This should include a regular time and place for daily practice. If they plan to use a recorded script, they can place the recording and playing device in the place where they plan to practice. Structuring and planning relaxation practice before participants leave the group may help to ensure adherence to these exercises. Reinforcement of relaxation practice continues to be critical!

STRESS MANAGEMENT: *Social Support and Reveiw of the Program*

Outline

- Review homework (10 minutes)

- Discuss social support (15 minutes)

- Discuss benefits of social support (5 minutes)

- Discuss obstacles to maintaining strong social support (10 minutes)

- Teach stress management techniques for maintaining social support (15 minutes)

- Review the program (5 minutes)

- Help group members form a personal plan for implementation (10 minutes)

- Distribute resource materials (5 minutes)

- Hand out Session and Program Evaluation Questionnaires (optional) (10 minutes)

Homework Review (10 minutes)

Discuss with group members what ways they have practiced assertiveness skills during the week. Have them describe situations in which they were able to make use of their new communication skills. Ask the following questions:

- "Have you been able to state wants and needs in 'I' statements?"

- "What listening skills have you used?"

- "Have you altered your body language in any way during interpersonal interactions?"

- "With whom are you practicing assertiveness skills regularly? With whom might you need to begin practicing these skills?"

- "Have you found that these skills are effective in reducing stress in your relationships?"

Understanding Social Support (15 minutes)

Personal and Material Resources

Ask group members what they think are their most valuable personal and material resources. Common responses are: car, house, intelligence, sense of humor, money, physical health, etc. The goal is to help group members realize that our social resources (i.e., our relationships with other people) often tend to enhance or detract from the importance that we place on these other personal resources. The following dialogue can help illustrate this point:

For example, having other people to share our accomplishments (e.g., degrees, new house, job promotion) with is often what makes us feel so good about them. Having others to console us during times of sorrow makes us feel less alone. Having someone to laugh with when we tell a joke lets us know that our humor is appreciated. Finally, having someone to share our thoughts and ideas with lets us know that we are both appreciated and beneficial to other people.

Receiving Social Support

Ask group members to indicate who in their social circle provides them with various types of support:

▪ Emotional (e.g., people who you can share with and cry with)

▪ Tangible (e.g., people who you can catch a ride from, borrow money from)

▪ Informational (e.g., people who can provide information or give advice)

▪ Affiliative (e.g., people who you can hang out and have fun with, who share the same views as yours)

Questions to ask the group include:

▪ "In what ways are these people able to provide us with support?"

▪ "Are these people available whenever we need them, or only occasionally?"

▪ "Are our interactions with others (even ones we love) always positive, or are they hurtful and disturbing at times?"

Giving Social Support

Ask participants to indicate the members of their social circle whom they provide with emotional, tangible, informational, or affiliative support. Ask group members how they think providing support to others indirectly helps themselves.

Explain that it seems that our willingness and ability to support others generally makes us feel good. Supportive individuals often have an increased sense of self-esteem and sense of purpose. Supportive people also have a reduction in feelings of helplessness and in feelings of guilt about receiving support (Zuckerman & Antoni, 1995).

Social Support Network Questionnaire

Have group members complete the Social Support Network Questionnaire in the workbook. This exercise will help them to identify where their support networks' strengths and weaknesses exist. After group members complete this exercise, facilitate a group discussion about what they found out about their support networks that they were not aware of before completing this exercise. Ask about those people in their social network who provide emotional, tangible, informational, and/or affiliative support. Ask where they noted strengths and where they perceived weaknesses across these domains.

Benefits of Social Support (5 minutes)

Supportive relationships can have health-promoting effects on both our mental and physical well-being. Ask group members to identify ways in which supportive relationships enhance their life and possibly promote their health. Address in the discussion the different kinds of direct and indirect benefits of social support.

Direct Benefits

Informational Support (e.g., from doctors, nurses, HIV-infected individuals)

- Promotes healthier behaviors

- Facilitates one's ability to obtain necessary medical care

- Helps plan optimal strategies for adhering to medication regimens

- Provides advice leading to solutions

Tangible Support (e.g., from friends and family)

- Helps accomplish chores

- Provides money to pay bills

- Provides assistance to meet various obligations

- Helps with transportation to medical appointments

Indirect Benefits

Emotional Support (e.g., from friends and family)

- As a coping resource, helps a person to redefine a stressor as being less overwhelming

- Reduces one's negative emotional reaction to events, allowing one to take positive actions

- Allows one to vent fears and to decrease private ruminations about stressors, thereby decreasing anxiety and depressed mood and possibly reducing stress hormone levels

Informational Support (e.g., from family, friends, HIV-infected individuals)

- Provides information that can be used to challenge irrational cognitive appraisals (e.g., catastrophizing, all-or-nothing thinking, etc.)

Tangible Support (e.g., from doctors and nurses)

- Helps with tasks that would be very difficult or impossible to accomplish on one's own (e.g., navigating the health insurance system for reimbursement for medical care)

Affiliative Support (e.g., from friends and family)

- Provides a sense of well-being, belongingness, purpose, and meaning

- Gives one a greater sense of personal control over life events

- May exert physiological effects, such as better-regulated stress hormone levels

Obstacles to Maintaining Strong Social Support (10 minutes)

Generate with the group a list of obstacles that might prevent people from establishing and maintaining a strong social network. If not mentioned by the group, add the following examples to the list:

- Multiple bereavements

- Sickness of friends, causing them to limit social activities

- Fractured family ties

- Self-imposed social withdrawal due to fears (of contagion, stigma, reminders of others who have gotten sick)

- Sense of disconnection from past pre-HIV life and relationships

- Other people fearing to be close (emotionally or physically) to an HIV-infected person

After generating this list of obstacles, engage in a discussion about them and the issue of controllability. Have participants rate the controllability of each obstacle with the group, on a scale of one (low control) to four (high control). See if group members disagree with each other in their controllability ratings of these obstacles, and allow them to challenge each other on this issue. Once they are more aware of these obstacles they can use cognitive restructuring to reframe the ways in which they are interpreting these perceived obstacles. In many instances they will find that by revising an overly strict, extreme, or rigid appraisal they will open themselves up to the possibility of using their assertiveness skills to enlist the support of others.

Stress Management Techniques for Maintaining Social Support (15 minutes)

Challenging Cognitive Appraisals

Discuss with the group how quite often, our own cognitive distortions get in the way of starting or maintaining healthy relationships with other people. Give examples such as the following:

For example, we may believe that other people won't like us once they get to know us, that people only seek out our friendship because they are after something, or that we are better off alone because people will always hurt us if we allow them to get too close.

Tell the group that challenging these kinds of erroneous thoughts and replacing them with healthier and more realistic cognitions is an important first step in allowing people to come into our lives and remain close to us over the course of time.

Use the following questions to stimulate a discussion about how group members' cognitive distortions prevent them from establishing and maintaining relationships that would add enjoyment to their lives.

- "What is your rationale for withdrawing from other people?"

- "How else might your family, friends, co-workers, and potential friends and partners react to you if you gave them a chance?"

- "How might you respond differently to people so as to gain their trust and improve your relationship with them?"

- "How might you be more open and honest with people about your life in an effort to increase your level of intimacy with them?"

Model of Awareness, Appraisal, Coping, and Resources

Figure 12.1 can be used to demonstrate the place of social resources in the stress management model.

Modifying Coping Strategies

The following coping strategies can be used as suggestions for dealing with a variety of stressors, including interpersonal stressors. These coping strategies involve your social network and include examples of both problem- and emotion-focused productive coping.

- Seek out information (as it relates to your medical condition)

- Seek out tangible aid (money, advice, instructions)

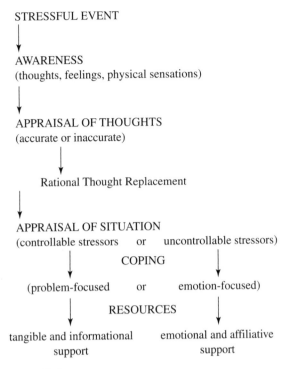

STRESSFUL EVENT

AWARENESS
(thoughts, feelings, physical sensations)

APPRAISAL OF THOUGHTS
(accurate or inaccurate)

Rational Thought Replacement

APPRAISAL OF SITUATION
(controllable stressors   or   uncontrollable stressors)

COPING

(problem-focused   or   emotion-focused)

RESOURCES

tangible and informational   emotional and affiliative
support   support

Figure 12.1

Model of awareness, appraisal, coping, and resources

- Communicate needs and feelings (positive and negative) more effectively to friends, family, and supportive others (e.g., medical personnel)

- Allow yourself to rely on trusted friends

- Enjoy the feelings of being nurtured by loved ones

- Express feelings (even anger) assertively

- Find a primary confidant (e.g. intimate partner, close friend, psychotherapist, support group, religious leader) and increase your connection to her

- Increase involvement in the community (lending support to others)

- Keep a journal of positive interactions you have had with others and how this made you feel

- Consider getting a pet

Steps to Support Network Modification

The following steps can be used as a guide for changing or improving aspects of one's social support network.

Step 1. Identify support network strengths and weaknesses.

Step 2. Rate the controllability of obstacles to forming and maintaining a network.

Step 3. Challenge cognitive appraisals blocking supportive connections.

Step 4. Modify and execute various coping strategies.

Step 5. Re-evaluate the situation to see if it has improved.

Review of the Program (5 minutes)

During the 10-week stress management program, group members learned a variety of techniques for increasing awareness of how stress affects their lives and ways that they can better manage their response to stressors. Briefly review these techniques and the goals of the program with the group.

Throughout the program, a primary goal has been the identification, or *awareness*, of stressors that group members commonly encounter, and the corresponding emotional, cognitive, behavioral, social, and physical symptoms of stress they typically experience as a result of these stressors.

The next step was to determine how thoughts, or *appraisals*, of stressors lead to various stress symptoms. Group members were introduced to the concept of cognitive restructuring as a strategy for changing distorted negative thoughts into more rational and realistic thoughts that would help them to perceive and think about the world in a healthier manner.

Several sessions were then spent examining coping strategies and determining where they serve group members well and not so well. Where participants were using less productive coping strategies, they began changing them to more productive strategies. The group also learned that problem-focused strategies might serve best in controllable situations but emotion-focused strategies might work better in uncontrollable situations. To help cope with other people, group members examined better ways to manage their anger and also learned how to express themselves assertively.

Finally, group members examined the important resources that they rely on in life, specifically social support. They considered how different people serve different support functions (tangible, informational, emotional, affiliative) and determined how they could improve their ability to establish and maintain strong social support networks.

Each of these goals was accomplished by introducing a variety of techniques designed to facilitate a certain component of stress management.

GOAL	TECHNIQUE
Awareness	PMR, body scan, meditation, breathing, imagery, autogenics
Appraisal	Cognitive restructuring
Coping	Productive coping skills, anger management, assertiveness
Resources	Social network, relaxation techniques

Each of these goals and activities is connected with the others, creating a complete stress management package that allows one to draw upon several strategies at once for managing a given stressor. Use the following dialogue to illustrate this point:

> *For example, individuals experiencing poor social support might simultaneously seek to build their awareness of how being socially isolated brings about various stress symptoms, examine how their distorted or negative thoughts prevent them from seeking out other people, determine how their passive coping strategies block them from solving interpersonal difficulties that keep them isolated, and finally examine how their social support network might be expanded and changed in ways to bring about more fulfilling interpersonal connections.*

Emphasize that for many stressors, employing several interconnected stress management techniques provides the most efficient strategy for dealing productively with problems and finding healthier solutions. Use the model of CBSM in figure 12.2 on page 168 to demonstrate how these techniques can be used by individuals living with HIV.

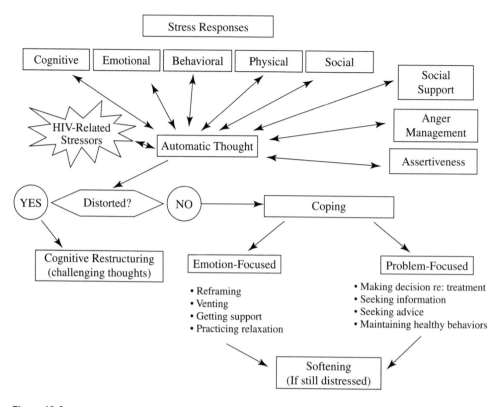

Figure 12.2

Model of CBSM for HIV-infected individuals

Personal Plan for Implementation (10 minutes)

Congratulate group members on completing the program. Reinforce their accomplishments and thank them for their participation. Emphasize that to maintain "stress management fitness" group members must continue using the techniques learned in this program, just as they would have to continue exercising to maintain physical fitness. Use the following points and questions to lead a discussion about implementation and maintenance of a personal stress management program:

■ "How do you plan to integrate stress management into your life?"

■ "Do you see yourself as able to call upon the stress management tools you've learned?"

■ "Are you able to envision a regular program of relaxation?"

■ "How will you begin this week? What tools will you use?"

Maintenance Meetings

Make a schedule of monthly maintenance meetings and encourage group members to come to them regularly. At these monthly meetings participants can expect camaraderie and support, discussions of progress, relaxation demonstrations, and review of the tools they learned during the program. At each of these monthly maintenance sessions, conduct a relaxation exercise of the participants' choice. Review those stress management techniques participants have used in the past month; when, where, and with whom they used them; any difficulties they have had in executing these techniques; and those they found to be most and least useful. Deal with any difficulties participants had in finding the time to practice relaxation and work with them to structure a maintenance plan.

Materials to Distribute at the End of the Session (5 minutes)

- Packet of Daily Self-Monitoring Sheets for the coming month (Or direct participants to photocopy from their workbooks or download multiple copies from the Treatments *ThatWork*™ Web site at www.oup.com/us/ttw)

- A 3- or 6-month calendar showing maintenance meetings and other noteworthy events (e.g., Gay Pride March, AIDS Walk)

- List of support groups, AIDS organizations, physicians and psychotherapists, religious organizations, community agencies, etc. (Create this list by gathering information relevant to your community. Group members might also contribute to this list by suggesting other resources that they think might be useful to others)

Session and Program Evaluation (optional) (10 minutes)

See example of Session Evaluation Questionnaire at the end of chapter 3. This questionnaire can also be adapted to evaluate the entire program.

References

Antoni, M. H. (2003a). Stress management effects on psychological, endocrinological and immune function in men with HIV: Empirical support for a psychoneuroimmunological model. *Stress, 6,* 173–188.

Antoni, M. H. (2003b). Stress management and psychoneuroimmunology in HIV infection. *CNS Spectrums, 8,* 40–51.

Antoni, M. H., Baggett, L., Ironson, G., August, S., LaPerriere, A., Klimas, N., Schneiderman, N., & Fletcher, M. A. (1991). Cognitive behavioral stress management intervention buffers distress responses and immunologic changes following notification of HIV-1 seropositivity. *Journal of Consulting and Clinical Psychology, 59,* 906–915.

Antoni, M. H., Caricco, A., Duran, R., Spitzer, S., Penedo, F., Ironson, G., Fletcher, M. A., Klimas, N., & Schneiderman, N. (2006). Randomized clinical trial of cognitive behavioral stress management on HIV viral load in gay men treated with HAART. *Psychosomatic Medicine, 68*(1), 143–151.

Antoni, M. H., Cruess, D., Klimas, N., Maher, K., Cruess, S., Kumar, M., Lutgendorf, S., Ironson, G., Schneiderman, N., & Fletcher, M. A. (2002). Stress management and immune system reconstitution in symptomatic HIV-infected gay men over time: Effects on transitional naïve T-cells (CD4+CD45RA+CD29+). *American Journal of Psychiatry, 159,* 143–145.

Antoni, M. H., Cruess, D., Klimas, N., Maher, K., Cruess, S., Lechner, S., Carrico, A., Kumar, M., Lutgendorf, S., Ironson, G., Fletcher, M. A., & Schneiderman, N. (2005). Increases in a marker of immune system reconstitution are predated by decreases in 24-hour urinary cortisol output and depressed mood during a 10-week stress management intervention in symptomatic gay men. *Journal of Psychosomatic Research, 58,* 3–13.

Antoni, M. H., Cruess, D., Wagner, S., Lutgendorf, S., Kumar, M., Ironson, G., Klimas, N., Fletcher, M. A., & Schneiderman, N. (2000).

Cognitive behavioral stress management effects on anxiety, 24-hour urinary catecholamine output, and T-cytotoxic/suppressor cells over time among symptomatic HIV-infected gay men. *Journal of Consulting and Clinical Psychology, 68,* 31–45.

Antoni, M. H., Esterling, B., Lutgendorf, S., Fletcher, M. A., & Schneiderman, N. (1995). Psychosocial stressors, herpesvirus reactivation and HIV-1 infection. In M. Stein & A. Baum (Eds.), *AIDS and oncology: Perspectives in behavioral medicine.* Hillsdale, NJ: Erlbaum.

Antoni, M. H., Lutgendorf, S., Ironson, G., Fletcher, M. A., & Schneiderman, N. (1996). CBSM intervention effects on social support, coping, depression and immune function in symptomatic HIV-infected men [Abstract]. *Psychosomatic Medicine, 58,* 86.

Antoni, M. H., Schneiderman, N., & Penedo, F. (2007). Behavioral interventions: Immunologic mediators and disease outcomes. In R. Ader, R. Glaser, N. Cohen & M. Irwin (Eds.), *Psychoneuroimmunology* (4th ed., pp. 675–703). New York: Academic.

Antoni, M. H., Wagner, S., Cruess, D., Kumar, M., Lutgendorf, S., Ironson, G., Dettmer, E., Williams, J., Klimas, N., Fletcher, M. A., & Schneiderman, N. (2000a). Cognitive behavioral stress management reduces distress and 24-hour urinary free cortisol among symptomatic HIV-infected gay men. *Annals of Behavioral Medicine, 22,* 29–37.

Barlow, D. H. (2004). Psychological treatments. *American Psychologist, 59,* 869–878.

Beck, A. T., & Emery, G. (1979). *Cognitive therapy of anxiety and phobic disorders.* Philadelphia, PA: Center for Cognitive Therapy.

Bensen, H. (1976). *The relaxation response.* New York: Avon.

Bernstein, B., & Borkovec, T. (1973). *Progressive relaxation training: A manual for the helping professions.* Champaign, IL: Research Press.

Burns, D. (1981) *Feeling good: The new mood therapy.* New York: New American Library.

Carrico, A., Antoni, M. H., Duran, R., Ironson, G., Penedo, F., Fletcher, M. A., Klimas, N., Spitzer, S., Llabre, M. & Schneiderman, N. (2006). Reductions in depressed mood and denial coping during cognitive behavioral stress management with HIV-positive gay men treated with HAART. *Annals of Behavioral Medicine, 31,* 155–164.

Davis, M., Eshelman, E., & McKay, M. (1988). *The relaxation and stress reduction Workbook* (3rd Ed.) Oakland, CA: New Harbinger.

Esterling, B., Antoni, M., Schneiderman, N., Ironson, G., LaPerriere, A., Klimas, N., & Fletcher, M. A. (1992). Psychosocial modulation of antibody to Epstein-Barr viral capsid antigen and herpes virus type-6 in HIV-1 infected and at-risk gay men. *Psychosomatic Medicine, 54,* 354–371.

Folkman, S., Chesney, M., McKusick, L., Ironson, G., Johnson, D., & Coates, T. J. (1991). Translating coping theory into intervention. In J. Eckenrode (Ed.), *The Social Context of Stress* (pp. 239–260). New York: Plenum.

Folkman, S., & Lazarus, R. S. (1980). An analysis of coping in a middle-aged community sample. *Journal of Health and Social Behavior, 21,* 219–239.

Institute of Medicine. (2001). *Crossing the quality chasm: A new health system for the 21st century.* Washington, DC: National Academy Press.

Ironson, G., Antoni, M., & Lutgendorf, S. (1995). Can psychological interventions affect immunity and survival? Present findings and suggested targets with a focus on cancer and human immunodeficiency virus. *Mind/Body Medicine, 1*(2), 85–110.

Ironson, G., Field, T., Scafidi, F., Hashimoto, M., Kumar, M., Kumar, A., Price, A., Goncalves, A., Burman, I., Tatenman, C., Patarca, R., & Fletcher, M. A. (1996). Massage therapy is associated with enhancement of the immune system's cytotoxic capacity. *International Journal of Neuroscience, 84,* 205–217.

Ironson, G., Friedman, A., Klimas, N., Antoni, M., Fletcher, M. A., LaPerriere, A., Simoneau, J., & Schneiderman, N. (1994). Distress, denial and low adherence to behavioral interventions predict faster disease progression in gay men infected with human immunodeficiency virus. *International Journal of Behavioral Medicine, 1*(1), 90–105.

Ironson, G., Lutgedorf, S., Starr, K., & Costello, N. (1989). *Anger management skills training,* Unpublished manuscript. University of Miami, Coral Gables, FL.

Kiecolt-Glaser, J. K., Glaser, R., Strain, E., Stout, J., Tarr, K., Holliday, J., & Speicher, C. E. (1986). Modulation of cellular immunity in medical students. *Journal of Behavioral Medicine, 9,* 5–21.

Kiecolt-Glaser, J. K., Glaser, R., Williger, D., Stout, J., Messick, G., Sheppard, S., Ricker, D., Romisher, S. C., Briner, W., Bonnell, G., & Donnerberg, R. (1985). Psychosocial enhancement of immunocompetence in a geriatric population. *Health Psychology, 4,* 25–41.

Lazarus, R. S., & Folkman, S. (1984). *Stress, appraisal, and coping.* New York: Springer.

Lechner, S., Antoni, M. H., Lydston, D., LaPerriere, A., Ishii, M., Stanley, H., Ironson, G., Schneiderman, N., Brondolo, E., Tobin, J., & Weiss, S. (2003). Cognitive-behavioral interventions improve quality of life in women with AIDS. *Journal of Psychosomatic Research, 54,* 253–261.

Leserman, J. (2003). HIV disease progression: depression, stress and possible mechanisms. *Biological Psychiatry, 54*, 295–306.

Lutgendorf, S., Antoni, M. H., Ironson, G., Klimas, N., Kumar, M., Starr, K., Cleven, K., McCabe, P., Fletcher, M. A., & Schneiderman, N. (1997). Cognitive-behavioral stress management decreases dysphoric mood and herpes simplex virus-Type 2 antibody titers in symptomatic HIV-seropositive gay men. *Journal of Consulting and Clinical Psychology, 65*, 31–43.

Lutgendorf, S., Antoni, M. H., Ironson, G., Starr, K., Costello, N., Zuckerman, M., Klimas, N., Fletcher, M. A., & Schneiderman, N. (1998) Changes in cognitive coping skills and social support mediate distress outcomes in symptomatic HIV-seropositive gay men during a cognitive behavioral stress management intervention. *Psychosomatic Medicine, 60*, 204–214.

Mason, J. (1985). *A guide to stress reduction.* Berkeley, CA: Celestial Arts.

Mulder, C. L., Emmelkamp, P., Antoni, M. H., Mulder, J., Sandfort, T., & de Vries, M. (1994). Cognitive-behavioral and experiential group psychotherapy for HIV-infected homosexual men: A comparative study. *Psychosomatic Medicine, 56*, 423–431.

Mulder, N., Antoni, M. H., Emmelkamp, P., Veugelers, P., Sandfort, T., van der Vijver, F., & de Vries, M. (1995). Psychosocial group intervention and the rate of decline of immunologic parameters in asymptomatic HIV-infected homosexual men. *Journal of Psychotherapy and Psychosomatics, 63*, 185–192.

Schneiderman, N., Antoni, M., Ironson, G., LaPerriere, A., & Fletcher, M. A. (1992). Applied psychosocial science and HIV-1 spectrum disease. *Journal of Applied and Preventative Psychology, 1*, 67–82.

Yalom, I., & Greaves, C. (1977) Group therapy with the terminally ill. *American Journal of Psychiatry, 134*, 396–400.

Zuckerman, M., & Antoni, M. H. (1995). Social support and its relationship to psychological physical and immune variables in HIV infection. *Clinical Psychology and Psychotherapy, 2*(4), 210–219.

About the Authors

Michael H. Antoni, Ph.D., is Professor of Psychology and Psychiatry and Behavioral Sciences at the University of Miami and Program Leader at the Sylvester Comprehensive Cancer Center, and has been a licensed psychologist in the State of Florida since 1987. Dr. Antoni leads the Bio-behavioral Oncology, Epidemiology, Prevention and Control research program, which includes over 20 faculty from the departments of Psychology, Psychiatry, Epidemiology, Medicine, and Microbiology/Immunology working together on transdisciplinary research projects. Dr. Antoni also serves on the graduate faculty in both the Clinical Health Psychology doctoral program and the Cancer Biology doctoral program at the University of Miami.

Dr. Antoni has led multiple NIMH-funded randomized controlled trials examining the ability of group-based cognitive behavioral stress management (CBSM) interventions to enhance psychological adjustment and modulate immune system functioning and health outcomes in HIV-infected men and women. He also serves as co-director of an NIMH pre- and post-doctoral training program in behavioral immunology and AIDS. He is also director of the National Cancer Institute (NCI)-funded Center for Psycho-Oncology Research (CPOR), one of the five mind-body centers funded by the NIH at the turn of the century. In the CPOR he directs a set of coordinated clinical trials and core laboratories that examine the effects of CBSM on psychosocial, endocrine, and immune functioning and the development of cervical carcinoma in women infected with HIV and human papillomaviruses (HPV) and on quality of life, endocrine and immune processes, and health status in women with breast cancer and men with prostate cancer. He has also served continuously as Principal Investigator for the past 14 years on an NCI-funded program of research in breast cancer that has demonstrated the efficacy of CBSM in three different randomized trials.

He has published over 380 journal articles, abstracts, chapters, and books in the area of stress management and health psychology, including *Stress Management for Women with Breast Cancer*. He is associate editor of the *International Journal of Behavioral Medicine* and *Psychology and Health* and serves on the editorial boards of *Health Psychology, Brain, Behavior and Immunity*, and *Annals of Behavioral Medicine*.

Gail Ironson, M.D., Ph.D., is Professor of Psychology and Psychiatry at the University of Miami and is a Board Certified Psychiatrist. She received her Ph.D. from the University of Wisconsin and her M.D. from the University of Miami, followed by residency training in Psychiatry at Stanford. She has over 150 publications in the areas of behavioral medicine, Psychoneuroimmunology, stress and coping with chronic illness (especially HIV), and examining psychological and biological factors that protect the health of people with HIV. She has been P.I. (Principal Investigator), Project Leader, or Co-P.I. on NIH-funded grants continuously for the past 18 years since she finished her residency training. A significant part of her research has been involved with implementing and examining the effects of cognitive-behavioral stress management with Mike Antoni and Neil Schneiderman in HIV. She also set up and has co-directed the Trauma Treatment program at the University of Miami for the past 10 years.

Notable accomplishments also include being President of the Academy of Behavioral Medicine Research in 2002 and being awarded the Alumni Professor Award for outstanding scholarship and teaching by the University of South Florida (Tampa). She is or has been on the editorial boards of five journals (*International Journal of Behavioral Medicine, AIDS and Behavior, Health Psychology, Journal of Applied Psychology, Journal of Disaster Psychiatry*). She is currently the recipient of two NIH-funded R01s ("Psychobiological Processes and Health in HIV" and "Efficacy of an Emotional Disclosure Intervention in HIV") and a grant from the Templeton/Metanexus foundation to study spirituality in HIV.

Neil Schneiderman, Ph.D., is James L. Knight Professor of Health Psychology, Psychiatry and Behavioral Sciences, and Medicine at the University of Miami. He is Director of the University's Behavioral Medicine

Research Center and Director of the Division of Health Psychology in the Department of Psychology. Dr. Schneiderman is the Director of both an NIH Program Project and a Research Training Grant from the National Heart, Lung and Blood Institute on biobehavioral bases of cardiovascular disease risk and management. He is also Principal Investigator of the NIH Multi-Center Hispanic Community Health Study as well as an NIMH Research Training Grant on psychoneuroimmunology and HIV/AIDS. Dr. Schneiderman has led multiple randomized controlled trials examining the effects of group-based cognitive-behavioral stress management on psychological adjustments and biological outcomes in the areas of HIV/AIDS, prostate cancer, and cardiovascular disease and has published more than 300 refereed articles. His honors include Distinguished Scientist Awards from both the American Psychological Association and the Society of Behavioral Medicine and the Outstanding Scientific Achievement Award from the International Society of Behavioral Medicine.